POTTERS OF SOUTHERN AFRICA

To Hans Boyum

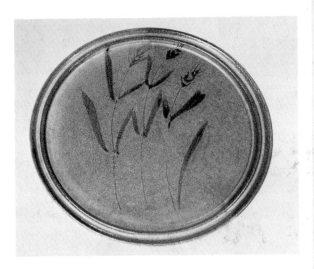
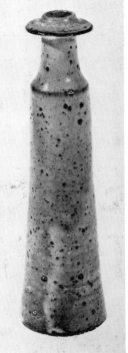

POTTERS OF
SOUTHERN AFRICA

G. CLARK   L. WAGNER

C. STRUIK (PTY) LTD
CAPE TOWN AND JOHANNESBURG 1974

C. STRUIK (PTY) LTD
Africana Specialist and Publishers

First edition 1974

ISBN O 86977 046 2
Library of Congress catalog card no. 74-82877

Designed by Al Todd Studios, Cape Town
Lithographic reproductions by Messrs Hirt and Carter (Pty) Ltd, Cape Town
Printed by ABC Press (Pty) Ltd, Cape Town
Bound by The Standard Press Ltd, Cape Town

CONTENTS

ACKNOWLEDGEMENTS

The authors wish to gratefully acknowledge the assistance of the potters, all of whom gave generously of their time, as well as the many others who have contributed towards this book. In particular we wish to record our thanks to Prof. Walter Battiss, Helen de Leeuw, Anneen and Hans Fransen, Ferdinand Haenggi, Shirley Lewis-Barr, Tim Maggs, Caril and Louis Martyn, Joelle Newton-Woof, M. J. Strydom, Breggie Wagner, Reg Wessels and the managements of Binnehuis, Cape Town and Craft Corner, Cape Town. A special thank you is due to Tim and Marlene Morris for their constant encouragement and unfailing optimism.

PREFACE

Compounded of the elements of earth, fire and water, pottery remains perhaps the most fundamental of the crafts. That is probably why, as a reaction against our materialistic and hyper-technological age, the last decade or so has seen an upsurge of interest in this ancient craft. This is manifested not only in the great number of people throughout the world who are endeavouring to become potters (the recently formed Association of South African Potters already has a membership of five hundred), but also in the increased awareness of the ordinary public of the enjoyment to be derived from possessing and using a good hand-made pot.

Possessing and using are two aspects of the experience of pottery which in the true connoisseur become one. The definition of 'using' is here extended beyond the literal sense of drinking out of a cup or cooking in a casserole to embrace the aesthetic response, both visual and tactual to a good pot.

There is a lot of twaddle talked about pottery as art, or pottery as craft, and there is a growing preciousness in some potters who feel that prestige is only to be found in high prices and gallery exhibitions. This may have the unfortunate effect of putting the potter beyond the reach of his most sympathetic and understanding public and consigning his work to the rarified world of the objet d'art, divorced from the reality of everyday.

I do not mean to decry collecting as such, for there is no doubt that the collector is responsible for the preservation of many a fine piece that might otherwise have been lost. It is also very satisfying for the potter who has struggled to gain recognition to find that his work can at last command a good price. What is a sad reflection on today's values however, is that art (and in this I include the potter's art) is too often reduced to a commodity on the stockmarket, bought for prestige and investment, rather than for the enjoyment of its intrinsic value.

Bernard Leach once defined pottery as an exploration of space. The true potter makes a statement, often profound, of his experience. He succeeds, as any artist does, when he transmits this to his perceptive public.

In *Potters of Southern Africa* Clark and Wagner present an objective study of fourteen potters or pottery workshops, supported by fine photographs. I would have liked to see included in the selection the work of Lily Pinchuck whose strong, direct and honest approach won her a Brickor Award in 1974.

Helen de Leeuw

INTRODUCTION

The discussion of pottery, like most areas of creative endeavour, is a semantic minefield. Some term their pots sculptures. Others become positively outraged at the suggestion of anything quite so esoteric as art intruding on their craft. At the one end of the spectrum is the ceramic engineer of Germany and Scandinavia, concerned with technical achievement to the exclusion of all else, while at the opposite end, one has the extreme left of the avant-garde in America and parts of Europe.

In South Africa, the situation is slightly simpler. Broadly, potters in the Republic can be grouped into two schools. The first is the traditionalists, acknowledging as their leaders potters such as Bernard Leach, Shoji Hamada, Raymond Finch and Michael Cardew. Their artistic expression is introspective, with the self sublimated in favour of impersonal perfection. The traditionalist as often as not binds his craft and life philosophy into a single purist entity, seeking seclusion rather than further stimuli, concentrating on the repetitive, perfecting a technique, a shape, a decoration, a glaze.

The other school is 'expressionist', for want of a better term. Venturing again into that minefield in search of definition, we find that these are the artist-potters rather than the craftsman-potters. To them the craft is a means of an innovative, personal self-expression. The style here is extrovert.

At the time of writing, the dominant school is still that of the traditionalists. The reason is historical. Whereas the potters in this field such as Bosch and Rabinowitz, have been producing and setting the norms of public taste since the late Fifties, the expressionists only began to emerge during the late Sixties. At this stage of pottery development in South Africa, it is probably premature to make too definitive a division into separate schools as a majority of working potters do have much in common.

The pottery movement in South Africa began to develop initial form and stature with the return to this country of Esias Bosch. As this is too brief a span to provide a valid perspective, it is important to look at the development of the artist or studio potter in Europe, as it is from there that we drew our belated influences.

Pottery first developed its 'art consciousness' in France during the mid-1800's. This was the product of a broader movement that resulted in the Art Nouveau period; a rebellion against decadent neo-classicism and the decline of aesthetic values that came with early industrialisation. It was natural that craft, being the counterpoint to mass production, should come to the fore.

Many men who previously would have been considered as nothing more than artisans, from potters Théodore Deck, Emile Lenoble, Emile Decoeur to glassworker Emile Gallé and jeweller René Lalique, were now revered as artists.

Theirs was not a merely arbitrarily conferred status. It was the result of craftsmen taking an artist's view and philosophy and striving to innovate and imbue their work with individuality. The first flowering of the French studio potters came with the 1867 Paris Exhibition and soon the pioneers were joined by others. The movement spread slowly in Western Europe, but caught on rapidly in Scandinavia, where it had a lasting effect.

This was a period of extravagant experiment (some valid, some not), as the potter, liberated from the confines and norms of his craft, groped for his identity. He worked with thick running glazes, both simple and elaborate forms, and used acid baths to achieve required textures.

The movement was a long time in reaching the British shores. Admittedly, great potters have produced highly individual work throughout the history of English ceramics, with Thomas Toft as one of the more outstanding early examples. The William Morris group influenced some potters in the late 1800's towards the philosophy of the French studio potters and the Royal Doulton factory sold signed individual pieces from the Lambeth School of Art in an attempt to popularise art pottery.

These influences were fragmented and regional and could never be graced with the description of being a movement. Britain had to wait until Bernard Leach returned from his studies and teaching in Japan before contemporary pottery was to acquire real importance.

William Murray, who had begun his experiments in stoneware in 1915, was influenced strongly by Shoji Hamada who came to Britain with Leach. The three potters, Shoji Hamada and Leach through their craft community in St Ives, and Murray at The Central School of Art, had a remarkable effect on standards and lifted the craft from the mediocrity of traditional village pottery. All three sold their work in galleries at high prices. It was only when the early pressures of the depression Thirties began to be felt that Leach turned to utilitarian pottery.

Leach had spent eleven years studying and working in the East, mainly in Japan. His apprenticeship as a potter began in 1911 under the representative of the seventh generation of the Kenzans. The head of the Kenzan 'school', founded by Ogata Kenzan, famous in the 1700's for his wide use of colour and the breadth of his calligraphy and brushwork, chooses the best pupils to use the name, palette and glazes of the master. When Leach arrived at St Ives on the Cornwall coast he carried with him the signal honour and responsibility of being the seventh generation to carry forward this tradition, together with his friend the late Kenkichi Tomimoto.

Leach brought with him the metaphysical craft philosophy of the Orient. He rejected the industrial-age division of labour and only accepted a pot as an individual piece of work if the potter had dug the clay, processed it, prepared his own glazes and then fired the finished work himself. His views were popular throughout the Twenties when a reverence of the crafts was considered an intellectual pursuit.

The Thirties were not kind to the potters. Leach's influence had become too widely accepted and most pottery had developed a 'family resemblance' to his work. This coupled with a flood of low-priced oriental pottery, soured the market. The prices that could be achieved did not justify the effort. Winch-combe was one of the few studios to survive the Depression while Leach was forced to retreat to Japan for some years.

After the war the influence of Leach became more strongly challenged by a new breed of artist-potters, most notably the 'English-Germans', Lucy Rie and Hans Coper. Very rapidly the community of art potters broadened with the work of populist Kenneth Clark, Ruth Duckworth's sensitive organic pottery and the hand-built excitement of Gillian Lowndes.

In America the post-war transition was far more radical, although the effect of this on South African pottery has been minimal. Only few potters in the Republic have studied in America. One of these is Marietjie van der Merwe, but the influence of Laura Andreson, her tutor, was not towards the iconoclastic, almost anti-pottery style that is now popular in America, but rather the purist Scandinavian approach. Another is Alice Heystek who spent several years working in South Africa before returning to America to settle. However her influence has been largely technical rather than aesthetic.

Our strongest influences are those of the Leach school, through Bosch, Rabinowitz and Gerlings who are devotees of this traditional frugality. Bosch's mentor was Michael Cardew who, in turn, is Leach's most successful student. Andrew Walford on the other hand, after a brief romance with Scandinavian design, has become progressively more involved in the Japanese School, inspired directly by Shoji Hamada, thought by many to be the world's greatest living potter.

Tribal African pottery, attractive as it is, has understandably not had much effect or influence on any of the White potters, as the culture is alien and the work aesthetically and technically limited. Only the Rorke's Drift pottery has been able to produce a contemporary African style, using traditional forms and decorations as a foundation. Thaba Bosigo has attempted this to a lesser extent, but the work does not have the clarity and strength of Rorke's Drift where potters are free artists.

There has been little experiment in pottery by artists whose natural home is in other media. One of the few examples, the ceramic mood pieces by Hannatjie van der Wat who is one of the country's leading hard-edge painters, is included in this book. Overseas, many of the top international artists, dating back to Gauguin, Rodin and later Picasso, Miro and Chagall, have worked in ceramics.

To the traditionalists, the artist using clay instead of a canvas is a blasphemy of the craft and, according to Leach, can never be valid even when attempted by a master like Picasso. Yet these ceramic pieces of work are taken seriously by students of the arts and not only for their 'freak' value.

What is a disturbing feature of the ceramic arts in South Africa is that given the buoyant market conditions, the pottery community has become strangely static. Instead of a wealth of new young potters, there is a vacuum, with the number of significant full-time potters emerging in the first three years of this decade adding up to no more than two or three. Yet four ceramic art departments exist in the art schools around the country and each year up to twenty-five students emerge after three years of intensive study of both the design and technology of ceramics. Of the potters presented in this book only three studied pottery at these institutions, one part-time, one full-time and the other not completing his course. Measured against the cost of running the departments, this can only be described as an appalling waste. The indictment is clear: something is very wrong with the method of teaching if these expensive installations have over the last twenty years produced only three artist-potters. Discussions at length with students reveal a distinct lack of pragmatism in the training. Because of the conditions prevailing in South Africa, it is essential that the students emerge fully capable of setting up and running their own studios.

This is necessary as, unlike Europe and America, there is almost no opportunity to become apprenticed to an established potter. The use of African assistants is partly economic and partly an effective means of keeping competition down, since the Africans lack the correct cultural, economic or social conditions to break away and set up on their own. A few students gravitate to the commercial pottery factory, but most end up behind typewriters, teller's desks and at the municipal craft schools.

Turning from the problems of the potters to those of the collector, it is obvious, from the work shown in this book, that pottery is an exciting and stimulating field. What is more, its collection is well within the reach of even the most modest budget. But, as with all fields of collecting, it must be approached with a certain amount of knowledge and with some caution if the work is one day to be of artistic or investment value.

Looking first at the least important aspect, that of investment, pottery in this country is not yet strictly a 'good buy'. Appreciation in value is not automatic. It is more likely that the initial re-sale value will drop after purchase. This is due to ruling aesthetic canons, as well as market structure.

Firstly, South African pottery has been dominated by table-ware and the muted art of the traditional potters. The collecting community has only now begun to realise that a piece of art-pottery can have as much aesthetic value as a painting or, a more closely related medium, sculpture.

Secondly, the market structure is not sympathetic. There is only one specialist pottery gallery. It is small, off the beaten track and, while run with enthusiasm and integrity, does not have the influence of the bigger city galleries. Of these, only one promotes pottery actively. That is Ferdinand Haenggi's Gallery 21 which represents Esias Bosch. The other outlet is The Craftsman's Market, the shop founded by Helen de Leeuw some twenty years ago, where she created a meeting-point between the artist and the market.

But there are signs of change. Art critics are now taking the work of our better potters seriously and reviewing them together with the rest of the art scene. The indications overseas, from the sales reports of Christie's and Sotheby's, are that the artist-potter has been 'discovered' by the art collector. Already an active market has developed in the pre-Forties studio pottery and prices are doubling from one year to the next. This is having a salutary effect on the price of current production by the leading international potters.

That this move will rub off on these shores is undoubted. As paintings, sculptures and even graphics recede further beyond the reach of all but the few, pottery will move up to fill the void. It is all a matter of time and education.

This book is intended to assist potters, students of the visual arts and collectors alike, in gaining an appreciation of the aesthetic values of pottery in Southern Africa. The choice of potters and their work has been dominated by the intention of including a representative range of practising potters in the country. It is not and was never intended to be a directory of all potters. To a degree selections have been personal, which was inevitable if the book was to make a statement.

One potter, who is not included in this book, but who deserves special mention for his contribution to the craft in South Africa, is the ebullient Sammy Liebermann. The studio that Liebermann started in 1955 has grown into a factory and the taste that his distinctive cream and brown earthenware created for simple rustic pottery made it easier for the potters who followed him to become established. Some, like Andrew Walford, served valuable apprenticeships with him. Liebermann was also one of the founder-forces behind the establishment of The Craft Potters Association which now has a membership of over four hundred in the Transvaal, its own quarterly magazine and a busy programme of exhibitions and events.

Comments attributed to potters in the following chapters are, with a degree of editorial licence, exact. They give an indication of the personalities, views and techniques of individuals at a point in their careers and are valid as such. But it must be appreciated that words are not their natural medium of expression. It is to their finished products that one must look for their true eloquence because therein lies the honest and lasting statement for which this book strives.

ESIAS BOSCH

**1 Stoneware plate with ash glaze and iron oxide decoration in red, pale brown and blue-grey, fired to 1 350° C
Diam. 41 cm**

THE DEVELOPMENT of Esias Bosch as a potter has followed a steady, unswerving upward curve.

En route, he has shed the tea-pots, sugar basins, casseroles and simplified ornamentation of his earlier days. The form and design of his work has altered too, with the long, tall shapes and wide lips of his earlier work largely sacrificed for a more pleasing sense of spatial economy. His growth to the stature of our master potter has been evolutionary rather than revolutionary.

'When I throw a pot or bowl,' he says, 'I know what the form will be. It may alter slightly to compensate for the characteristics of the clay, but merely to sit and produce in the hope that something good will emerge, is a waste of time.' To him shapes are not made – they evolve from one to the other and only with positive concentration can something be made.

Born on July 11, 1923 near Winburg in the Orange Free State, Bosch took a course in fine arts at the University of Witwatersrand. He then went on to obtain a teacher's diploma from the Johannesburg Technical College Art School where he achieved a distinction in portraiture. His interest in pottery was late in awakening, spurred on by a three year scholarship of which he spent one year at the Central School of Art, London, and the remaining years working in various studios. At the Central School of Art he had the privilege of working under Dora Billington, considered to be one of the best teachers at the time. His practical apprenticeship began with Raymond Finch in Winchcombe at one of the few pottery studios to survive the ravages of the Depression in the Thirties. Here he learnt much about glazing and decoration and with Raymond Finch he produced the first stoneware at Winchcombe. Finally he moved to Cornwall where he worked with Michael Cardew.

**2 Two stoneware vases with wood ash glaze fired to 1 350° C
Height 23 cm**

**3 Three large stoneware pots with incised decoration in wet clay. On the left an iron glaze, and the other two pots glazed with a dolomite glaze
Tallest pot is 110 cm**

4 Assembling large panels
for the Schlesinger Centre

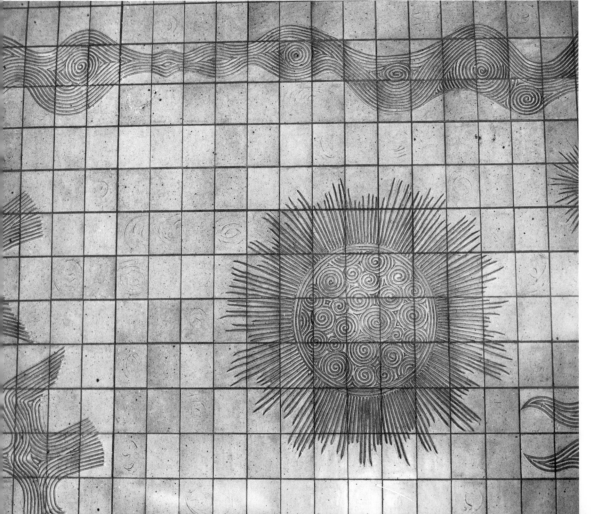

5 Detail from stoneware
mural at Jan Smuts
Airport. Large tiles
with high relief drawn
on with strips of clay
while wet and dolomite
glazed
Size 57,9 m x 6,4 m
1972/3

ESIAS BOSCH

6 Stoneware vase, raw glazed
with pine ash glaze
and reduction fired to 1 300° C
Height 36 cm   1967

Bosch arrived back in South Africa in 1952, teaching in Durban for two years before moving to Pretoria. For some time he worked in earthenware, building up a small but loyal following. The beginning was difficult. In 1962, after a visit by his mentor, Cardew, he made the transition to stoneware. Looking for both seclusion and economy, he eventually acquired a rocky outcrop of land from a farmer in White River near the Kruger National Park. The harsh, almost aloof surroundings appealed to Bosch, as did a local supply of four-foot wattle logs to fire the large kiln he had built.

Esias Bosch's workshop in White River is rather large for one person, but he needs much room when he makes large murals. Making pots alone does not always satisfy him. He feels that in pots one is too limited in scale and in textural qualities which can only be brought out in murals. Bosch sees the making of murals as a challenge to the potter since industry cannot always produce individual architectural work. Two of his works that demand special mention can be seen in the foyer of the Schlesinger Building in Braamfontein and the huge mural in the International Departures Hall of Jan Smuts Airport. Here the artist emerges with force and clarity, combining the purism, economy and technical perfection of his pottery with a free, fresher expression.

Initially Bosch's output was prodigious. Helen de Leeuw recalls that on one of her visits to his studio he threw 30 casserole dishes in half an hour. The fruits of his kiln pioneered interest in this country for simple, clean-lined stoneware. Bosch, the man, made as great an impression as his work and his integrity and high standards at last created a norm for pottery in South Africa, discrediting those who tried to fob off their kiln disasters and running treacle glazes as being 'artistic'.

Today Bosch still produces full-time, but he tends to spend more time in making his pots. He produces little tableware and concentrates on decorative vases, lidded jars, large pieces and murals. His work is dominated by an insistent concern for technical excellence. He prefers to work in raw materials which he grinds himself. To him the fresh and honest quality of a pale granite or ash glaze appeals more than the rather 'clever' coloured glazes. He has worked mainly with ash glazes and a granite glaze while his attention is also turning to salt glazes.

Now using an oil kiln, Bosch throws or slabs all his work. A feature is the scale on which he works, turning pots of a metre or more on the wheel, producing vast slab plates and large lidded jars. In his small lidded bowls with their delicate, enamel-bright, oxide designs, the touch of the perfectionist is clearly apparent. The lid design is repeated not only inside the bowl, but underneath the lid and on the foot as well. Large pieces are decorated with a sense of economy. At one stage throwing rings were just visible, applied subtly to give interest to the expanses of the glaze. Now attractive linear sgraffito designs are applied with considerable effect. The bases are finished simply by patting them until slightly concave. Pottery to Bosch is an extension of life. In both, a sense of frugality and control is evident. Much of his attitude is summed up in one of those eloquent statements by Bernard Leach which Esias Bosch is fond of quoting: 'The pot is the man, his virtues and vices are shown therein, no disguise is possible.'

Bosch would like to see a very good school of ceramics in South Africa, independent of any institutions, where students can begin at the beginning with less emphasis on academic theory and fewer sophisticated aids. It is possible that he may one day offer his studio for the establishment of such a school.

8 Slabbed stoneware piece with brown oxide over a white semi-matt wood ash glaze
Height 37 cm   1972/3

9 Stoneware slab pot with brown iron saturated glaze
Height 35 cm   1973

7 Unpacking the small salt-glaze kiln

10 **Early stoneware piece with brown decoration painted on the dark green glaze and fired in a wood kiln to** 1 280° C
Diam. 25 cm 1968/9
Coll. T. Maggs

11 **Wood ash glazed stoneware with iron and cobalt design, reduction fired to** 1 350° C
Height 11 cm 1973

ESIAS BOSCH

12 **Left: Raw glazed stoneware with incised design under off-white matt glaze**
Height 60 cm   1972/3

13 **Above: Raw glazed stoneware with incised design under a white dolomite glaze**
Height 45 cm   1972/3

14 **Top right: Stoneware with an incised design under an off-white matt glaze, raw glazed and reduction fired to 1 350° C**
Height 75 cm   1972/3

15 **Right: Raw glazed stoneware with incised design and a matt glaze, speckled due to iron in the clay**
Height 44 cm   1972/3

16 Stoneware lidded jar with iron and clay glaze
Height 30 cm   1971

17 Stoneware vase with granite and clay glaze
Height 30 cm   1970

19 **Very early stoneware piece ash glazed in tones of brown**
Height 120 cm 1970
Coll. F. Haenggi

18 **Packing the trolley kiln**

20 Square stoneware dish
with ash glaze and iron
decoration
Width 56 cm   1974

21 Slab-built stoneware box
with off-white matt glaze
and iron and cobalt design,
reduction fired to 1 350° C
Height 30 cm   1969
Coll. T. Maggs

22 Stoneware with applied design and dolomite glaze, reduction fired to 1 350° C
Height 25 cm   1973

23 Stoneware covered
dishes with incised
decoration over wet clay
and a celadon glaze,
reduction fired to 1 350° C
Height 11 cm, 14 cm   1973

SONJA GERLINGS

SONJA GERLINGS was born on January 29, 1942. Her interest in pottery stems from her childhood associations and contact with Audrey Frank. Later she spent three years studying graphics at the Michaelis School of Art and then became apprenticed to Hym Rabinowitz. She worked with him for three years before setting up on her own.

Sonja Gerlings works at Zeekoevlei on the outskirts of Cape Town. The studio is a cramped shed, in which she somehow manages to accommodate herself, the wheel and an electric kiln. She is the only potter in this book working in low-fired earthenware and shows none of the inadequacy or self-consciousness that other potters seem to associate with this medium.

She describes the last seven years that she has been working on her own as having been difficult, yet she has no intention of changing her circumstances. She follows a strict daily working routine that begins early in the morning. Her output is relatively small and sold through one selected outlet in the Western Cape. Except for exhibitions, her work is seldom seen anywhere else in the country.

Sonja Gerlings is an artist who acknowledges traditional roots. This shows in the succesful decoration which is both muted and sensitive. Mostly the designs are soft-edged, giving an almost 'out-of-focus' quality to her pieces. Especially distinctive of her brushwork, which derives from Oriental influence, are her fish and grasses designs. However, she has the ability to imbue even the most simple bowl with a fascination through her skilful use of colour and form. Sgraffito is another decorative technique in which she excels and in which she admits exercising exceptional patience to realise her intentions.

The Orient apart, her influence comes largely through the works and writings of Bernard Leach and Michael Cardew, yet it is difficult to label Sonja Gerlings as a member of any school. Her chosen background is traditional and most of her output conforms to this ideal. However, she can, when she chooses, work with a sense of creative self-expression as her ceramic sculpture illustrated in this chapter shows.

1 Coiled and unglazed earthenware figure on glossy ba
Height 44 cm 19

26

2 Slab-built earthenware with
shiny white glaze
Height 25 cm   1970

3 Thrown and hand built earthenware
with blue glaze over cobalt slip and
wax resist design
Height 20 cm   1969
Coll. T. Maggs

4 Grey matt glazed earthenware
with applied decoration
Height 32 cm 1971

5 Earthenware with applied, fingered and sgraffito
decoration under a golden-brown semi-gloss
glaze with an expanse of unglazed body at the foot
Height 32 cm   1971

6 Grey matt glazed
earthenware with
cobalt brushwork
Height 11 cm 1973
Coll. T. Maggs

7 Earthenware with golden
to dark brown glaze
Height 19 cm 1971

8 Earthenware plate with
a glossy white glaze and iron
and cobalt decoration
Diam. 25 cm   1974

9 Earthenware bowl with matt
iron-grey slip over wax
resist decoration
Diam. 14 cm   1973

10 Yellow ochre glazed earthenware with
iron pigment design and turquoise rim
Height 13 cm   1973

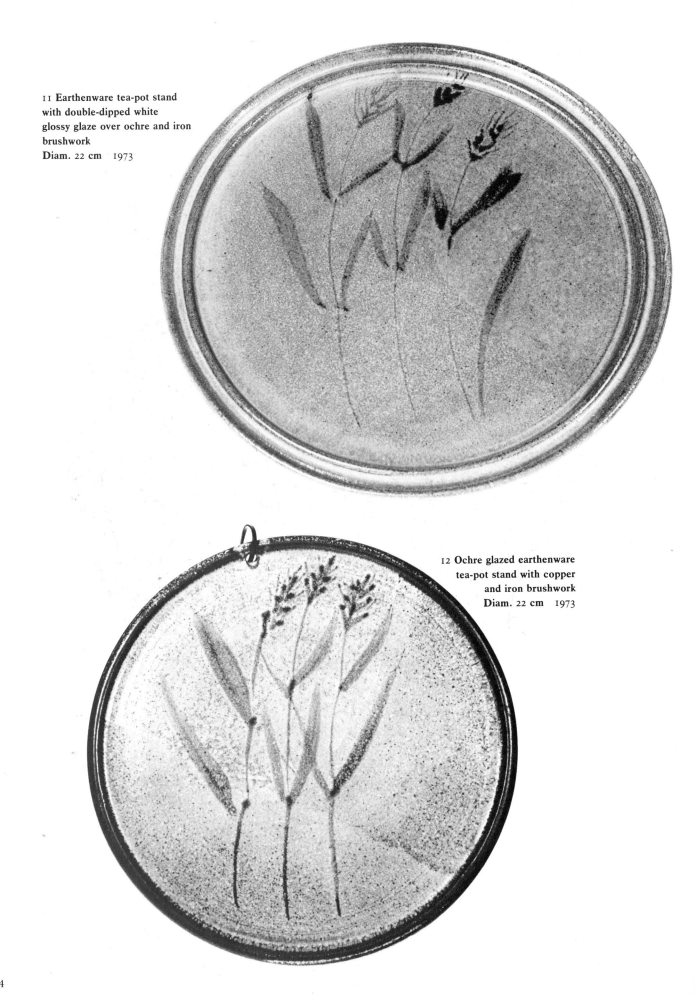

11 Earthenware tea-pot stand
with double-dipped white
glossy glaze over ochre and iron
brushwork
Diam. 22 cm 1973

12 Ochre glazed earthenware
tea-pot stand with copper
and iron brushwork
Diam. 22 cm 1973

13 Earthenware pilgrim bottle with
iron slip and sgraffito decoration
Height 30 cm   1974

14 Earthenware salt cellar and pot-pourri,
blue slip sgraffito under beige matt glaze
Height 7 cm

15 Golden-brown glazed earthenware,
darker on the shoulder and neck
Height 12 cm   1971

16 Earthenware.

pot, ochre glazed with iron oxide design
Height 12 cm

Salt & pepper cellars, blue slip sgraffito under beige matt glaze
Height 7 cm

ate, yellow ochre glaze with iron and cobalt brushwork
Diam. 33 cm

Bottle, cobalt slip with sgraffito under light brown glaze
Height 7 cm   1973

SONJA GERLINGS

17 Earthenware vase with a grey-blue matt glaze
Height 15 cm   1971

BRYAN HADEN

1 Stoneware with grey feldspathic
glaze and brushwork decoration
Height 44 cm 1974

MOST MEN are lucky enough to have one all-consuming passion in their lives. Bryan Haden has two; sailing and pottery. The siting of his self-built home and studio overlooking False Bay enables him to indulge and satisfy both. However, the fact that together with a thrower-assistant he processes and uses seven tons of clay a year, is indication enough as to which pursuit claims the most attention.

Haden is a modest, quiet-spoken man who does not intellectualize about himself or his work. He is interested in pottery as a traditional craft serving basic functional needs, and believes that 'pots are primarily containers; they should be reasonably priced and advertise their functions'.

Bryan Everard Haden was born in 1930 on the large family farm Bonnefoi in the district of Carolina, Eastern Transvaal. He grew up in a family of painters. His mother, Ruth Everard Haden, is one of the five members of the remarkable Everard-Haden group of women painters. After Haden had finished his schooling in Swaziland, he also decided to train as an artist, but to concentrate on pottery – though he is an accomplished painter as well. He studied pottery at Natal University in Pietermaritzburg under Hilda Ditchburn, and spent 1953 visiting potteries in England.

On his return he opened his first pottery studio in Pietermaritzburg, making oxidised stoneware in an electric kiln. His work was first exhibited at this time at the South African Craft Exhibition in Washington. In spite of a successful one-man show in Pretoria in 1957, he was forced to close his studio for financial reasons in 1959. For the next four years he tried his hand at other jobs, including art teaching in Rhodesia, where he met his wife, Heather.

In 1963, after their marriage, Haden opened his second pottery at Bonnefoi, but a year later he

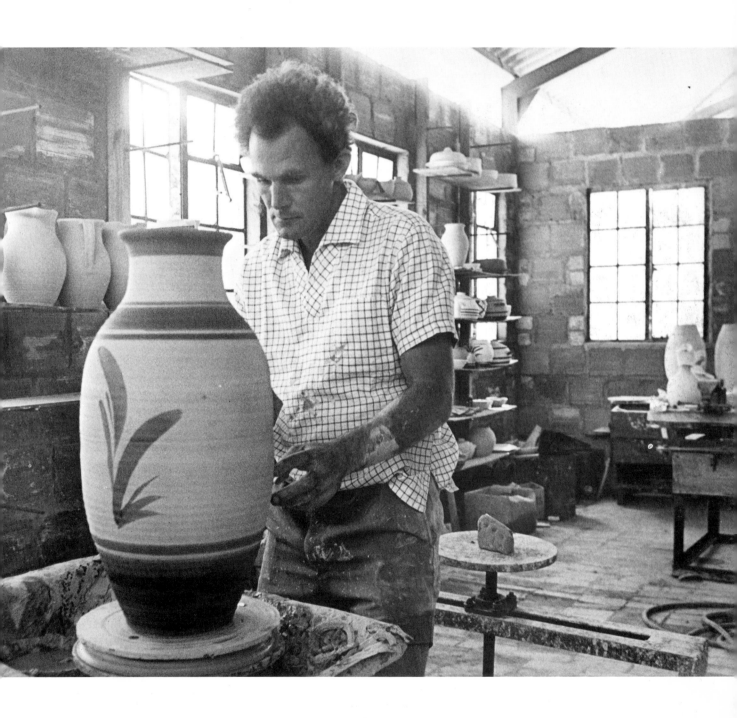

2 Celadon glazed stoneware bowl
with decoration in iron oxide pigment
Height 7 cm 1973

3 Stoneware casserole glazed on
the inside only
Height 17 cm 1974

4 Stoneware bowl with tenmoku glaze
and trailed-on white glaze
Height 12 cm 1972
Coll. P. J. Olivier Art Centre, Stellenbosch

BRYAN HADEN

returned to England where he worked at the well-known Aylesford Monastery Pottery. In 1965 the Hadens came to Cape Town. Haden taught at the Green Point Art Centre and decided to stay at the Cape. In 1966 he settled near Gordon's Bay, built his third studio and concentrated on stoneware.

His present studio is large enough for both the kiln and the clay preparation. He uses an oil-fired down-draught kiln with two oil burners. The clay preparation machinery includes a pugmill, blunger and filter-press. He and his thrower-assistant each use an electric wheel.

Bryan Haden produces mainly stoneware, but occasionally also porcelain. His pots are usually soft bisque-fired and then glazed in reduction. He uses stoneware glazes which he keeps as simple as possible. Pots are sometimes kept unglazed with glaze inlay decoration.

Like many other local potters he has been indirectly influenced by Oriental pottery through the work of Bernard Leach, and more recently he has become an ardent admirer of the work and ideals of Michael Cardew.

Haden works close to the simpler traditional shapes and concentrates on larger functional pieces such as casseroles, jugs, bowls and dishes. He is one of the few potters who can handle sizes of up to a metre; a vase of this height he throws in two or three sections.

His basic work has a rugged appeal and the robust strength of the honest craftsmanship in which he believes. But in his more personal pieces this robustness and vigour is balanced by a refinement of form and decoration which reveals the artist behind the craftsman and is the stamp of Bryan Haden's best work.

5 **Stoneware covered jar**
with decoration incised into wet clay.
The dolomite glaze is thicker
where it shows white
Height 37 cm 1970
Coll. P. J. Olivier Art Centre,
Stellenbosch

6 **Matt feldspathic glazed stoneware, decoration in wax with iron oxide pigment brushed over it**
Height 20 cm   1972
Coll. P. J. Olivier Art Centre, Stellenbosch

7 **Dolomite glazed stoneware**
Height 21 cm   1971
Coll. P. J. Olivier Art Centre, Stellenbosch

8 Matt dolomite glazed stoneware
Height 36 cm 1970
Coll. P. J. Olivier Art Centre,
Stellenbosch

9 Semi-matt feldspathic glazed stoneware lidded jug
Height 23 cm   1970
Coll. P. J. Olivier Art Centre,
Stellenbosch

10 Dolomite glazed stoneware
Height 21 cm   1974

BRYAN HADEN

11 Stoneware slab pot with dolomite glaze
over sgraffito decoration
Height 48 cm   1974

12 **Celadon glazed stoneware with iron oxide pigment decoration**
Diam. 40 **cm** 1974

13 **Dolomite glazed stoneware samovar**
Height 56 cm 1974

ALICE HEYSTEK

ALICE HEYSTEK could so easily have been a sculptor. A long fascination with the work of such sculptors as Henry Moore and Jean Arp certainly inclined her in this direction. She rationalises her bridging pottery and sculpture by admitting, 'It was no longer the functional aspect of the container as an end in itself which concerned me, but the use of the container as a means with which to express a sculptural idea'.

Alice Heystek was born on September 27, 1925 in Albany, New York. In 1946, she graduated from the New York State College of Ceramics at Alfred University with a degree in ceramic art and design. It was there that she met her husband Hendrik Heystek, a South African who was studying ceramic engineering and technology. On completion of their studies they moved to Pretoria where she taught ceramics in the Adult Education Department of the Pretoria Technical College. Alice Heystek eventually stopped teaching when the output of her studio increased. At that time she was producing mainly African and animal designs on a local earthenware clay. In 1953 she held her first one-man show at Van Schaik's Gallery in Pretoria.

In 1960, after 12 years in South Africa, her husband accepted a research post in California. The change of environment and the demands of her family briefly interrupted her career. With the youngest child at school she resumed work and from this point her empathy for hand building began to develop.

Alice Heystek found that the slow technique she

Stoneware wall panel. Brick clay blocks were produced from a brick extruder and the carving is 4 cm deep. Fired in a reduction atmosphere in a commercial brick kiln 1972
Ill. C. Skotnes

ALICE HEYSTEK

2 Stoneware pot decorated with black clay while still damp, bisque-fired and glazed with a high zinc glaze, later rubbed off the surface of the black clay decoration
Height 40 cm 1973
Coll. W. O. Heimann

developed as a variation of the coiling method satisfied her interest in sculpture. 'Often I would feel something occur during the making of a pot which seemed to be happening almost by itself. Hand building gave me time to understand what was evolving and to help it along.'

In 1970 they returned to South Africa where Hendrik Heystek became director of research at Brickor. Alice Heystek worked for several months in a corner of one of the brick plants, firing her pots in reduction brick kilns. Then the Heysteks bought a house and she built a studio and kiln. This kiln, fired with bottled gas, was a new design for South Africa.

She loves the asymmetry of organic forms and shapes which are tall and monolithic or low and wide with strongly swelling curves. They are often elliptical with an axis somewhat off the vertical and the openings are designed to express as much of the total curve as possible. Her glazes are developed from natural material. She is amazingly prolific in spite of the slow technique.

June 1973 found the Heysteks on their way back to the United States, this time Alabama where they are now settling. All her remaining pots were bought by a gallery in George. Alice Heystek feels that this moving to and fro between two continents has not dulled her interest in experiment. If anything, the problems of different raw materials and conditions have acted as stimuli to sustain her search for new techniques.

3 Stoneware pot rubbed with
iron oxide loaded glaze
resulting in an 'orange-peel'
texture and gun-metal colour.
Fired in reduction
together with sewer pipes
in a commercial salt-glaze kiln
Height 62 cm 1971
Coll. B. S. Kuming

4 Stoneware pot with a
once-fired granulated effect.
A dark slip was applied over
the wet clay, textured and dried.
A glaze rubbed into
the dry pot 'crawled' into
the pockets of the texture
Height 30 cm 1973
Coll. M. J. Strydom

ALICE HEYSTEK

5 Stoneware with dark clay circular decoration
Height 37 cm

6 Dark blue glazed stoneware
Height 45 cm

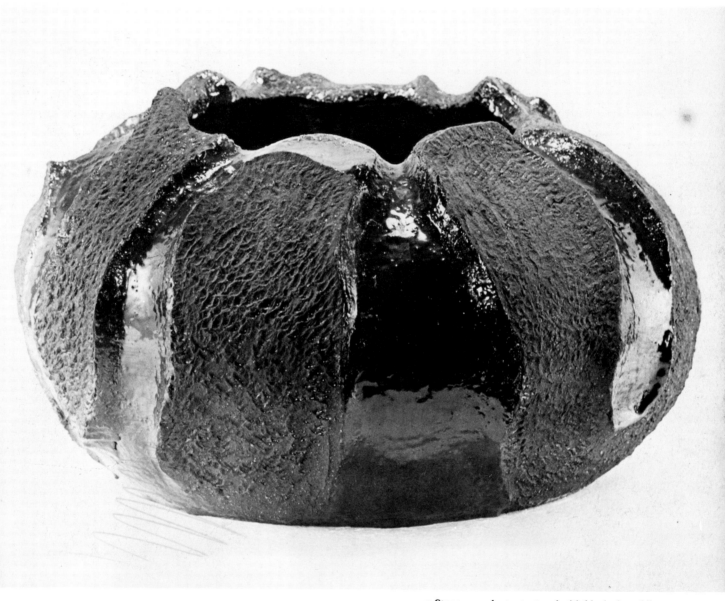

7 **Stoneware planter textured with black clay while**
wet and glazed with black glaze which was rubbed off
the textured surface for contrast
Height 27 cm 1973
Coll. G. Struik

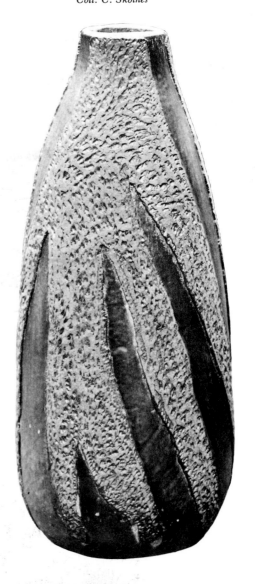

8 Stoneware pot fired in oxidation and
decorated while wet with a dark slip. The golden
iron glaze is rich in zinc and crystallizes out
at the correct temperature
Height 104 cm   1973
Coll. H. Harris

9 Stoneware decorated with dark clay,
then fired in oxidation with a blue glaze.
Glaze rubbed off the textured surfaces
Height 59 cm   1973
Coll. C. Skotnes

10 Stoneware pot poured
with white zinc glaze
and then sprayed with
a semi-transparent
glaze to reveal partially
the shapes of the pours
Height 40 cm   1972

11 Bisque-fired stoneware
pot glazed by pouring
varicoloured glazes
down the sides
Height 28 cm   1971
Coll. C. Skotnes

12 Stoneware entrance light
decorated around the
holes with dark clay
while wet. Glaze applied
after bisque-firing
and rubbed off the dark
clay areas
Height 19 cm   1973
Coll. W. O. Heimann

13 Double-glazed stoneware
pot. A high magnesium
glaze with a tendency
to 'crawl' was superimposed
on an iron saturated glaze
and reduction fired
to 1 300° C in a commercial
brick kiln
Height 36 cm   1971
Coll. C. Skotnes

14 Stoneware candle-holder with high zinc glaze
crystallized out into small dark gold crystals
Height 20 cm   1973

15 Stoneware with heavily modelled surface texture and dark slip-coated background. A semi-transparent glaze, with bluish cast where the glaze picked up iron from the slip, is partially rubbed off both the textured part and some of the dark areas
Height 27 cm 1973
Coll. H. Harris

16 Flat shape of this stoneware pot was inspired by the oyster shells found on the Durban beach. The clay wa coated with a dark slip when wet and cut away in a pattern along the edges. The usually opaque white glaze turns semi-transparent when reduction fired and iron in the slip gives an opalescent blue
Height 37 cm 1973

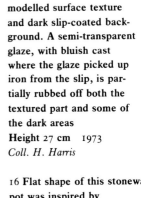

17 Stoneware pot made in one piece with ridge added
and lid cut when the pot was leather-hard.
The edges of the knobs were thickly loaded with
an iron saturated glaze and the gold colour
allowed to flow down the sides of the pot
Height 45 cm   1973

CHARLES GOTTHARD JACOBS

CHARLES GOTTHARD JACOBS was born on January 5, 1951 and grew up in Johannesburg.

For three years he studied at the Johannesburg College of Art and joined the ceramic class in his last two years for a course which was ostensibly in architectural ceramics. In fact, he learnt little about architecture, so little that his first mural crashed to the ground while he was trying to erect it!

College, whatever its shortcomings, was an effective spring-board. While there, he entered three ceramic sculptures (his first three), for the 1971 Brickor Exhibition. One was an intricate 'torso' composed of 250 stoneware jigsaw puzzle pieces. This was a difficult and clever piece of work which caused much discussion.

His work is exciting and individual. By South African standards it could be classed as avant-garde, although he does not try to break away from natural thrown shapes. Instead he distorts and magnifies them to create a dynamic interplay of lines and angles in his groups.

Jacobs works in a large studio at Honeydew, near Johannesburg. This, together with a 1,359m³ (48 cubic foot) down-draught gas kiln, was sponsored by a property development company for whom he undertook to erect a 10,033m² (108 square foot) mural – his first mural since starting on his own.

He uses a Walford designed wheel on which he greatly enjoys throwing. Jacobs likes using clay with a high grog content for the large work which he prefers. For more refined smaller pieces he mixes this with a white stoneware clay.

To Jacobs pottery is very personal. In his search for artistic authenticity and identity, he uses materi-

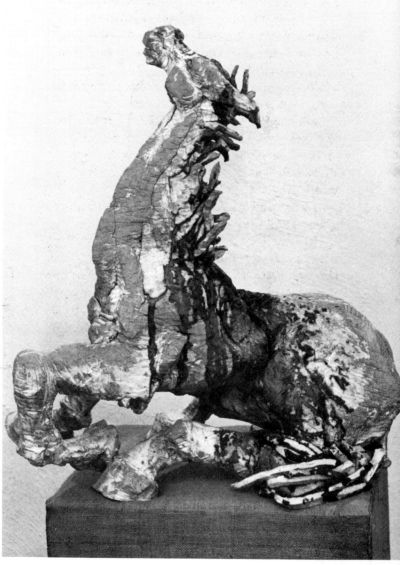

1 Hand built stoneware sculpture supported by a wooden armature, white matt glazed with copper on the mane and back. Fired in one piece to 1 220° C

Height 85 cm   1972

Coll. R. Diener

CHARLES GOTTHARD JACOBS

als which he feels are compatible with the subject, such as paint, soft sheets of hot perspex and thin layers of cork on the lids and sides of pots.

Each potter has his particular fascination. In Jacobs' case it is lids. In his so-called 'soldier pots', he has created a very original style with slabbed lids resembling the helmets of mediaevel warriors.

'What I set out to create here, as in all my work, is an expression of tension, reflected either through the angularity of the piece or through a conflict of positive and negative lines,' he says.

Despite his youth, he has a clear direction of purpose. Keenly interested in the work of other potters (particularly the American avant-garde school), he admits to only a few direct influences. These relate to a technical rather than an aesthetic point of view – such as Hans Boyum his science lecturer, and the potter, Alice Heystek.

Thrown stoneware group
'soldier' pots with slab-built lids
d green-brown glossy glaze
ed to 1 220° C. The necks are
ished with a thin layer of cork
eight 20 cm - 30 cm   1973
ll. C. G. Jacobs

Thrown stoneware group
'soldier' pots with slab-built lids
d a thin layer of cork on
e tallest pot for textural contrast.
on matt glaze reduction fired
1 220° C
eight of tallest pot 43 cm   1973

4 Thrown stoneware pot with
slab-built lid. Iron worked into
the clay gives speckled effect.
Transparent glaze fired to 1 200° C
Height 32 cm   1973

5 Partially glazed thrown
stoneware pot with thrown lid.
White glossy glaze fired
to 1 220° C
Height 25 cm 1973
Coll. C. G. Jacobs

6 Partially glazed thrown
stoneware group with hand built
slab lids, reduction
fired with iron saturated glaze
Height 16 cm - 20 cm   1973
Coll. Mrs Danziger

7 Thrown stoneware with slabbed
lids and iron saturated
glaze, reduction fired to 1 220° C
Height 15 cm - 26 cm   1973
Coll. C. G. Jacobs

CHARLES GOTTHARD JACOBS

8 Thrown stoneware with white crackle glaze and iron oxide
flakes, reduction fired in gas kiln to 1 200° C
Height 18 cm 1973

9 Thrown stoneware shape with sla
added to dented sides and glaz
with a transparent glaze w
iron oxide markings. Fired to 1 220°
Height 20

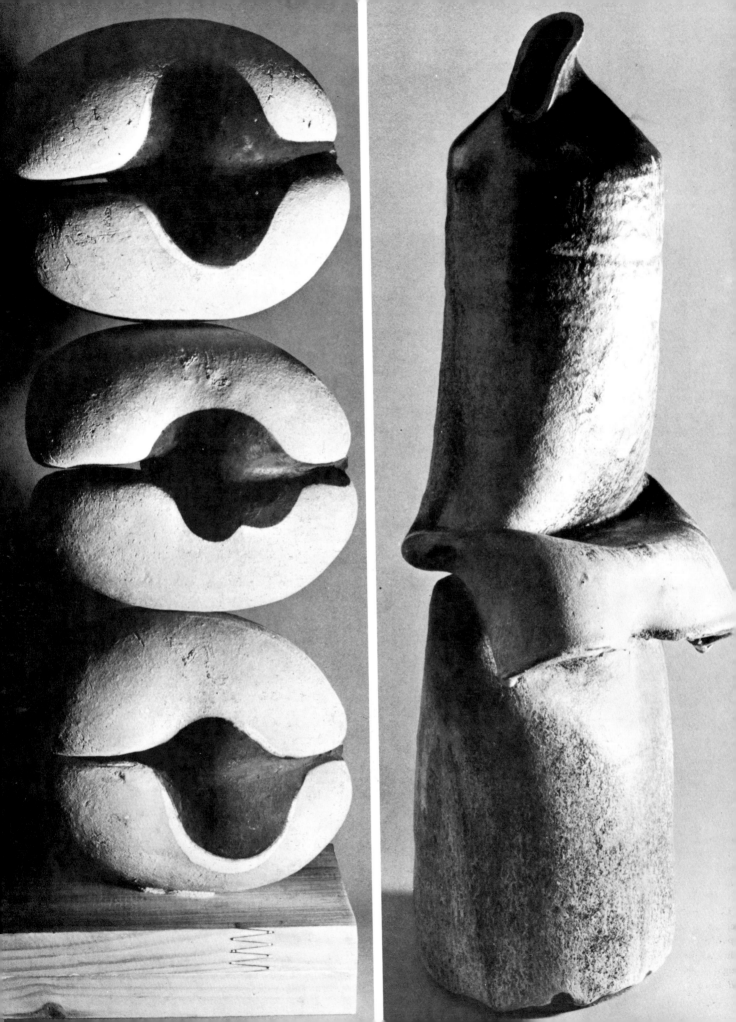

CHARLES GOTTHARD JACOBS

12 Slab-built stoneware pot with
thrown top and applied clay
letters, glazed with semi-matt
copper glaze and fired in gas kiln
to 1 220° C
Height 64 cm 1973
Coll. C. G. Jacobs

Far left: 'Coco de Mer' stoneware sculpture
h copper oxide design, press-moulded
m the giant seed and reduction fired
1 200° C
ight 80 cm 1973
l. C. G. Jacobs

Left: Stoneware pot thrown in two
tions, distorted and then assembled.
perimposed black and white matt glazes
luction fired to 1 220° C
ight 44 cm 1973
l. Gallery 73

KOLONYAMA

1 **Press-moulded stoneware plate reduction fired to** 1 300° **C.**
The red-black slip was quickly ladled on. A satin-white feldspathic glaze
gives colours ranging from brown to rust over the slip
Width 30 **cm** 1973

THE TRADITION of one of Britain's top potters, Raymond Finch, is alive and thriving in the foothills of Lesotho.

His son, Joe Finch, while visiting South Africa in 1968 to work with Esias Bosch, was approached to open a studio-production pottery in Lesotho. In May 1969, it was decided to convert seven grain silos at Kolonyama into a suitable building. Joe Finch, of Winchcombe Pottery in England, supervised the construction of a 2,831m³ (100 cubic foot) down-draught oil kiln and started to train the local Basuto as potters. He was joined by Trudi Pickford of the Farnham School of Art and together they were responsible for the development in the first eighteen months after which their first exhibition, consisting only of slab pots, was held in Cape Town.

Joe Finch attempted to instil at Kolonyama his father's philosophy of the highest standard at the lowest price. In this he has been largely successful. The Finch philosophy is an admirable one and helped the Winchcombe Pottery to survive the Thirties when the Depression closed numerous studios in Britain.

Joe Finch returned to England but Kolonyama was fortunate in that Raymond Finch offered to assist for a period. After six months he handed over to Malcolm Bandtock from the Harrow School of Art, London. Bandtock returned to Britain in 1972 and Bill van Gilder, also from the Harrow School of Art, came to Kolonyama to continue the process of management and teaching.

Kolonyama works in earthenware, stoneware and has recently begun trial production in porcelain using a body recipe by David Leach. The 'house' glazes are restricted to four standards; a satin white, celadon green, a honey-coloured and earthy brown glaze. Slip-trailed designs on the plates are distinctly Finch. For the rest the work relies on its attractive form and very controlled glazing for its effect. The salt glazing has been most successful, particularly in Van Gilder's own work. Van Gilder does a large amount of the throwing at Kolonyama and also works as a potter in his own right.

Kolonyama Pottery, with Bill van Gilder, has exhibited widely throughout South Africa and supplies a great number of craftshops across the country.

BILL VAN GILDER

2 Stoneware corked storage jar salt-glazed with flowing yellow ochre-based glaze inside
and dipped to the shoulder outside.
Reduction fired to 1 300° C producing a buff
to dark brown mottled surface
Height 15 cm   1973

3 Salt-glazed stoneware jug reduction fired
to 1 300° C
Height 24 cm   1973

4 Stoneware storage jars thrown individually. The light-coloured
jars are glazed with a speckled white matt glaze and decorated with
iron brushwork. The other three are glazed with a deep green
celadon glaze and iron and cobalt decoration. Reduction fired to 1 280° C
Height 8 cm 1973

5 Thrown and turned reduced stoneware platter, part of a three-piece
place-setting which is a standard line. The all over semi-matt saturated iron-
red glaze is decorated with a thick celadon glaze trailed pattern Diam. 22 cm 1973

6 Porcelain lidded box thrown in one piece and
needled apart while leather-hard, glazed
with semi-transparent celadon glaze over iron and cobalt
brushwork and fired to 1 300° C
Height 6 cm   1973

KOLONYAMA

7 Stoneware wall-plate glazed with saturated
iron-red glaze and decorated with green celadon
poured freely as a double glaze. Where the two
glazes overlap, a brown to black tenmoku results.
Raw glazed and reduction fired to 1 280° C
Diam. 36 cm   1973

9 Stoneware wall-plate with blue cobalt slip overglazed with a wood-ash glaze. The surface is partly matt and partly crystalline with a fine surface of gold flecks where slip and glaze meet. Reduction fired to 1 280° C
Diam. 36 cm 1973

8 Stoneware fruit dish with blue cobalt slip, white matt wood-ash glaze and combed decoration applied to slip. Tremendous colour variation ranges from yellow to gold to matt white and many tones of blue. Reduction fired to 1 280° C
Diam. 38 cm 1973

10 **Press-moulded stoneware plate
with red-black slip and feldspathic
satin-white glaze, reduction
fired to 1 300° C
Width 14 cm   1973**

11 **Reduced stoneware storage jars glazed
in semi-matt saturated iron-red glaze and
fired to 1 280° C. This is a standard line
produced at Kolonyama
Height 22 cm – 27 cm   1973**

12 Stoneware cruet set with deep cobalt slip beneath a white matt wood-ash glaze, reduction fired to 1 280° C. A blunt-toothed plastic comb is pulled through the slip for decoration. **Height 6 cm, 9 cm, 6 cm 1973**

13 Reduced stoneware storage jars glazed with saturated iron-red glaze and fired to 1 280° C. These jars are thrown in repetition and produced in a variety of sizes **Height 18 cm – 23 cm 1973**

14 Small covered porcelain box with light green celadon glaze
and iron and cobalt decoration, reduction fired to 1 250° C
Height 11 cm   1973

15 Light green celadon glazed porcelain with iron and cobalt
decoration, reduction fired to 1 250° C
Diam 8 cm   1973

C1 **WALFORD**
Stoneware tea-pot with semi-gloss glaze over
delicate oxide brushwork. Reduction fired
Height 18 cm
Coll. G. Clark

C2 **BOSCH** Glazed stoneware mural
Width 2,9 m Height 2,6 m   1974
Coll. W. Cohen

C3 **RABINOWITZ** Stoneware tile in oatmeal-coloured
feldspathic glaze, wax decoration and dipped in a tenmoku glaze
Area of tile 30 cm² 1972

C4 **BOSCH** Early stoneware pot fired in a wood kiln

C5 MARCUSON
Clear glazed porcelain bowl
with artificially reduced
copper-red and cobalt markings
Diam. 10 cm 1973
Coll. M. Finger

C6 KOLONYAMA
Moulded stoneware bottle
with satin-white glaze over
green oxide design
Height 23 cm
Coll. G. Clark

C7 **HADEN** Feldspathic glazed stoneware with
iron oxide pigment over wax patterning
Height 63 cm   1972
Coll. P. J. Olivier Art Centre, Stellenbosch

C8 **HADEN** Stoneware with feldspathic glaze,
decoration in iron and cobalt pigments
Height 62 cm   1973/4
Coll. H. D. Losinsky

C9 **VAN DER MERWE**
Porcelain bowl with foot. The bowl and foot were thrown separately, pinched and attached. A copper red glaze fired in reduction to 1300° C gave the cherry red colour with purple and blue
Height 18 cm   1970
Coll. M.v.d. Merwe

C10 **RABINOWITZ** Stoneware lidded jars and plate.
Plate with an oatmeal-coloured feldspathic glaze,
decorated in wax and then dipped in a tenmoku glaze
Plate diam. 26 cm   1974

C11 **MORRIS**
Stoneware tube vases
with iron slip on a
feldspathic glaze
Height 36 cm – 71 cm   1974

C12 **Group of stoneware
vases with dolomite and
celadon glazes**
Height 20 cm – 43 cm   1974

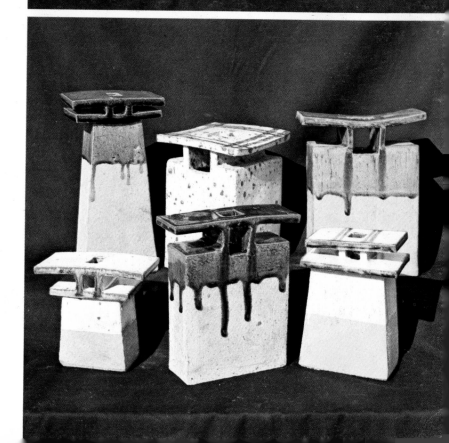

C13 **MARCUSON** Hollow stoneware eggs in brown stoneware
bowl. The eggs are handmade and glazed with speckled matt glazes
Diam. of bowl 36 cm, eggs 3 cm – 8 cm   1973

C14 **GERLINGS**
Ochre glazed earthenware
bowl with wax resist and iron
and cobalt decoration
Diam. 34 cm   1974

C16 **MARCUSON** Group of six
handmade stoneware cylindrical forms
Height 20 cm – 35 cm   1974

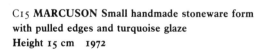

C15 **MARCUSON** Small handmade stoneware form
with pulled edges and turquoise glaze
Height 15 cm   1972

C17 **VAN DER MERWE**
Feldspathic glazed stoneware vase
with wax resist and iron decoration.
Reduction fired to 1300° C
Height 19 cm   1972
Coll. M. v. d. Merwe

C18 **HEYSTEK** Stoneware wall panel. Brick clay blocks were
produced from a brick extruder. Made to be artificially illuminated indoors
1972
Coll. B.S. Kuming

C19 **BOSCH**
Thrown and pressed stoneware
vase with salt-glaze
Height 23 cm   1972

C20 **MORRIS**
Stoneware plate, server,
bread bin and storage jars
Height of bin 46 cm   1974

C21 RORKE'S DRIFT
Hand built stoneware by Dinah Molefe
with applied clay and painted design
in iron and black slips under a
kaolin matt glaze. Some red clay was
added to the stoneware body
Height 30 cm 1973
Coll. E.L.C. Art and Craft Centre, Rorke's Drift

C22 RORKE'S DRIFT
Hand built stoneware by Ivy Molefe with
applied clay and sgraffito decoration and
painted iron and black slips under a kaolin
matt glaze
Height 37 cm 1974

C23 **GERLINGS** Ochre semi-gloss
glazed tea-pot with iron and
copper decoration
Height 15 cm 1974

C24 **BOSCH** Stoneware jar with lid. Blue iron glaze over
an incised decoration, reduction fired to 1350° C
Height 20 cm 1974

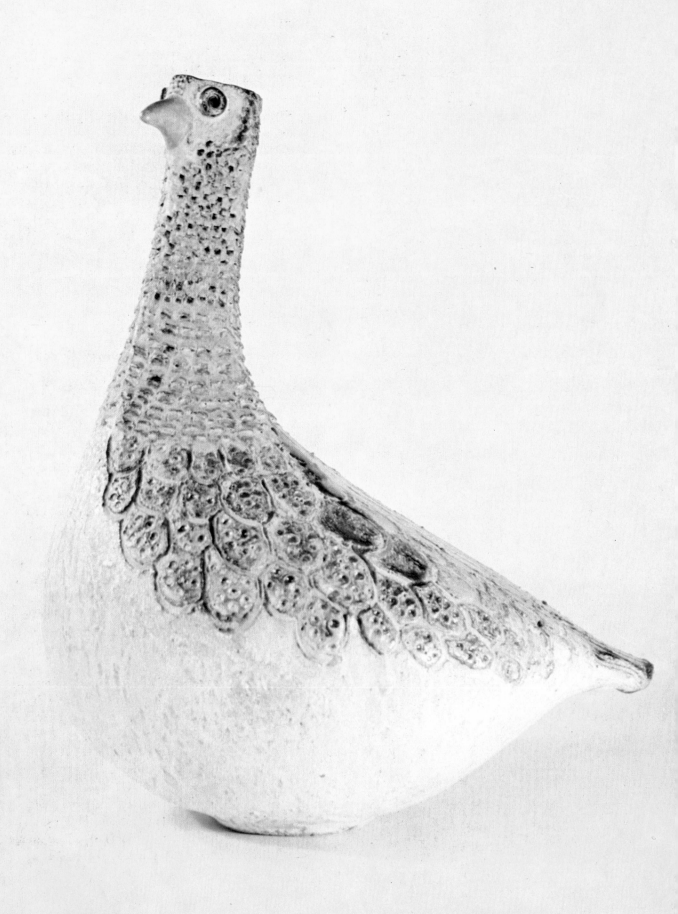

HELEN MARTIN

HELEN MARTIN is a catalyst.

Her name is associated with the careers of many of our top artist-potters, among them Tim Morris and Thelma Marcuson, as well as aspiring newcomers such as Hannatjie van der Wat, Ann Leader and Pat Lewis. But the sense of purism, which provides the driving impetus for her role as teacher, inhibits her output. She prefers the role of innovator to that of a repetitive craftsman. Not surprisingly, she has little rapport with the wheel although she throws with precision.

Helen Martin was born on November 13, 1942. She left Rhodesia to train at the St Martin School of Art, London, studying portraiture and fine arts. After two years she moved to the more intimate climate of Hammersmith College of Art where she took her national diploma in design, majoring in pottery and textiles. This was followed by a three month stint at the Rosenthal factory in Germany where she met the Finnish designer Tapio Wirkkala. He invited her to Finland and had a profound influence on the development of Helen Martin's perfectionist working philosophy. She then moved to Copenhagen and worked for a time at Saxbo, a small ceramics factory.

In 1964 she came to South Africa, choosing the long route on an east coast cargo ship. Helen Martin worked initially in industrial ceramics at Ferro-Enamels and then gained experience in the retail field with Helen de Leeuw before deciding to open her own studio.

A trip to the Cape to arrange for her clay supplies resulted in the chance meeting with Tim Morris, at Hym Rabinowitz' workshop. The two taught and worked together for almost two years in Orchards, Johannesburg. During this time Helen Martin also established a pottery school at the Patterson Park Recreation Centre.

After her marriage to Tony Dunstan, she set up a studio at her Gardens home. A serious motor accident and the arrival of a daughter have somewhat limited her output. Much of her energies are taken up with tending to a selective but busy private school that she runs, and in the training of apprentices at her new home in Westcliffe.

Her ceramic birds have provoked considerable artistic attention and collectors' interest. They are eloquent examples of her work, combining originality, discipline and a high standard of technical

5 Coiled stoneware 'bird-pot' with incised
sign and dolomite multi-glaze
ight 54 cm
l. H. van der Wat

HELEN MARTIN

achievement. These aloof pieces take up to three days to coil and sculpt, and the decoration may require a full week. Line and proportion are critical factors as the bird's contours must be effective from all angles.

Her studio is small, practical and compact. Clay is processed in a small adjoining yard where raw materials are mixed with the popular Crammix stoneware clay. Helen Martin prefers working in stoneware. Experiments in porcelain, such as her delicate blue and white birds, have been successful, but she does not enjoy working with this exacting body, maintaining that it is like 'building with water'.

Contact with other potters does not influence Helen Martin in the visual sense. When other potters or artists are mentioned in connection with her artistic development, their contribution is usually an intellectual one. This integrity is apparent in her attitude to exhibitions.

She says: 'To me an exhibition does not mean a lot of money in a short time, although this is rapidly becoming the norm. I see it not as a market-place at all, but as a theatre arena in which to say something with ones work. Moreover, what is said should be personal and original. So while I will continue to work and sell, I will not enter a gallery with a one-man exhibition until my statement is complete and valid.'

2 Coiled stoneware with incis
design and coloured dolom
glazes applied by bru
fired to 1 280
Height 47 cm   19

1 Coiled stoneware with incised
and applied design and brushed-on
coloured dolomite glaze
Height 52 cm

3 Stoneware pinch pot with
white glossy dolomite
glaze and multi-coloured
glaze effect
Height 23 cm   1969

4 Stoneware pinch pot glazed with dolomite,
brown glazes and oxides
Diam. 42 cm   1969

5 **Very dry volcanic dolomite glazed stoneware with blackened
excess oxide effect**
Diam. 35 cm 1969

6 Stoneware pinch pot with white
dolomite glaze. The high magnesium
content of the glaze caused the cobalt
rim to turn purple
Height 9 cm   1972
Coll. H. Martin

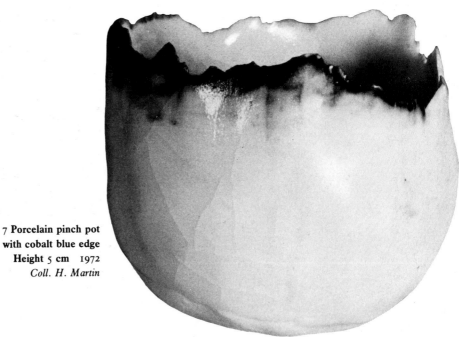

7 Porcelain pinch pot
with cobalt blue edge
Height 5 cm   1972
Coll. H. Martin

8 Coiled porcelain 'bird-pot' with white dolom
glaze and delicate touches of cobalt oxide, fired to 1 280°
Height 30 cm   19

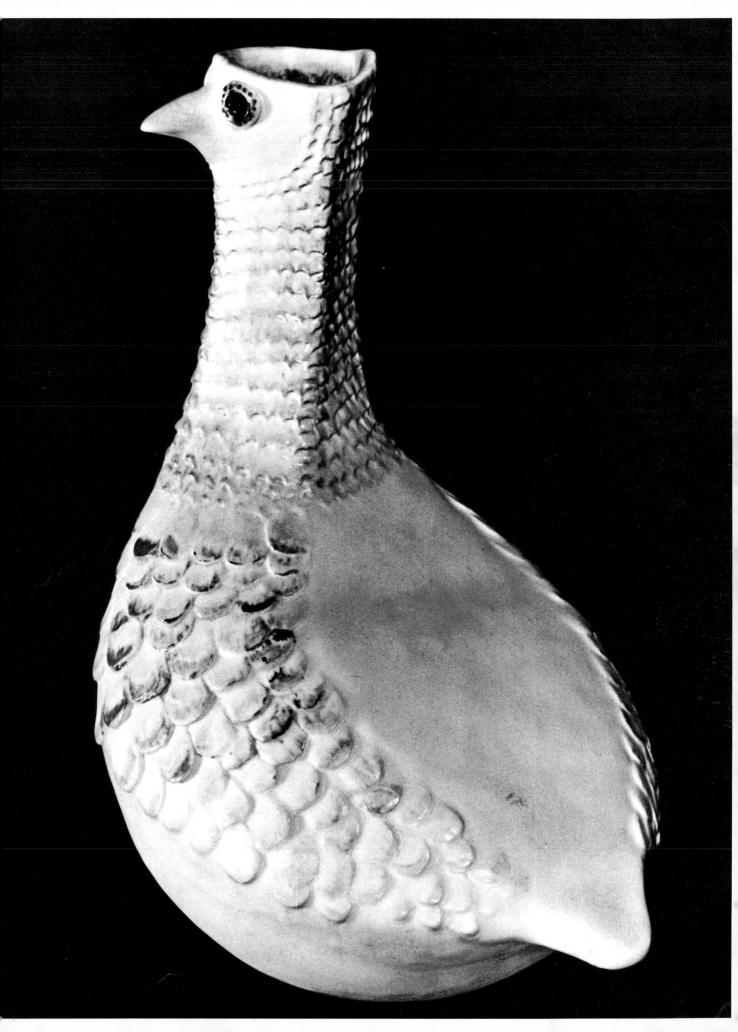

HELEN MARTIN

9 Slab-built stoneware, triple-dipped in
light and dark green, and black glazes
Height 16 cm   1970

10 **Stoneware, ash glazed with yellow ochre**
Height 14 cm, 21 cm   1973

11 Stoneware in foreground
double-dipped in dark green
and turquoise glazes
Height 15 cm, 18 cm   1973
Stoneware in background has
tan iron multi-glaze
Height 17 cm   1973

12 Thrown stoneware with thin white dolomite double glaze
Height 3 cm   1972

13 **Dolomite glazed stoneware with the high magnesium content of the glaze causing the cobalt edging to turn purple**
Height 12 cm   1970

THELMA MARCUSON

THELMA MARCUSON'S serious interest in ceramics started only ten years ago. Since then she has become accepted as one of the country's most accomplished potters. Pottery was the final destination in a path of exploration that took her through many media. Thelma Marcuson was seeking an artistic field in which she could achieve an acceptable level of perfection. Pottery proved to be the answer.

Thelma Marcuson was born in Johannesburg on July 13, 1919. She had little formal education in her craft. A two-year part-time course in ceramics at the Johannesburg College of Art was the foundation. There she studied under John Edwards who, she insists, could teach 'an orang-utang to throw'! This was followed by private lessons in glaze technology. She progressed, learning as much as she could from the many practising potters with whom she became friends. Such was her sense of purpose and tenacity that, in some cases, she overtook her mentors and has built up a formidable technical knowledge.

The output of her studio is small. Occasionally she makes tableware, but this is the exception. Once a design has been perfected it is rarely repeated, usually discarded in favour of new fields of exploration. Although Thelma Marcuson does throw large pieces from time to time 'to keep up with the boys', as she laughingly refers to it, her best work is her small pinch pots and other youthfully organic and earthy forms.

Her move into porcelain has been successful, creating particularly distinctive porcelain lidded boxes which are a mere 4 cm high. Porcelain is her métier because of its technological challenge.

She finds the science of being a potter exciting and her studio is crammed with the results of hundreds of glaze tests. Each experiment is carried out with the purpose of achieving improved control of her glazing as she is little impressed with chance successes in the kiln.

Thelma Marcuson is unashamedly eclectic and derivative both in her work and her inspiration. Following a recent trip to America, her attention has now turned to crystalline glazes. Overseas travel has

1 Three thrown porcelain forms with m
glaze over combed pale lilac engo
Diam. of smallest bowl 12 cm 19

108

THELMA MARCUSON

played a major role in establishing her sense of design.

She works in a neat, comfortable studio housed in two rooms in the garden of her Dunkeld home in Johannesburg. One room contains two medium-sized electric kilns in which she fires both stoneware and porcelain. Assistance comes from her ex-gardener, Hendrik Mmatau, who has now been promoted to full-time duties in the studio and carries out some of the slabbing and clay processing.

Thelma Marcuson has the advantage that she does not have to depend on her studio for a living. She is free to concentrate more on experiment than output. Standards are high: no seconds are allowed to leave her studio. As a collector herself, with an extensive collection of international ceramics, she understands only too well the artistic standards which must be maintained – and rigorously adheres to them.

**2 Pale grey porcelain bowl
with cobalt brushwork
Diam. 16 cm 1974**

**3 Porcelain bowl with
matt glaze over combed
pale lilac engobe
Diam. 16 cm 1974**

4 Pinched, pulled and scraped unglazed stoneware egg-shell forms
Height 16 cm   1973

5 Fine stoneware ovoid glazed duck-egg blue and filled
with pulled and engraved organic fungal interior forms
Width 18 cm   1972

7 **Hand built double-edged stoneware with matt blue-grey glaze and sgraffito markings**
Diam. 13 cm 1973
Coll. G. Clark

6 **Hand built flattened stoneware vases in various shades of tan**
Height 15 cm – 20 cm 1972

THELMA MARCUSON

8 Hand built, cut and stacked
stoneware slabs with light
blue-grey glaze
Height 20 cm, 14 cm   1972
Coll. P. Goldberg

9 Slabbed stoneware
pot with added layers
of thinly rolled clay.
Grey-green matt glaze
Height 23 cm   1973

10 Porcelain (David Leach body) thrown boxes with clear glaze and engraved and applied decoration
Height 4 cm – 5 cm   1973

11 Below left: Porcelain box with engraved design on lid under a clear glaze
Height 5 cm   1973

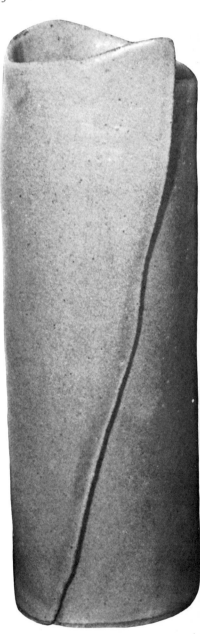

12 Left: Thrown porcelain with pulled handle and clear glaze
Height 7 cm   1973

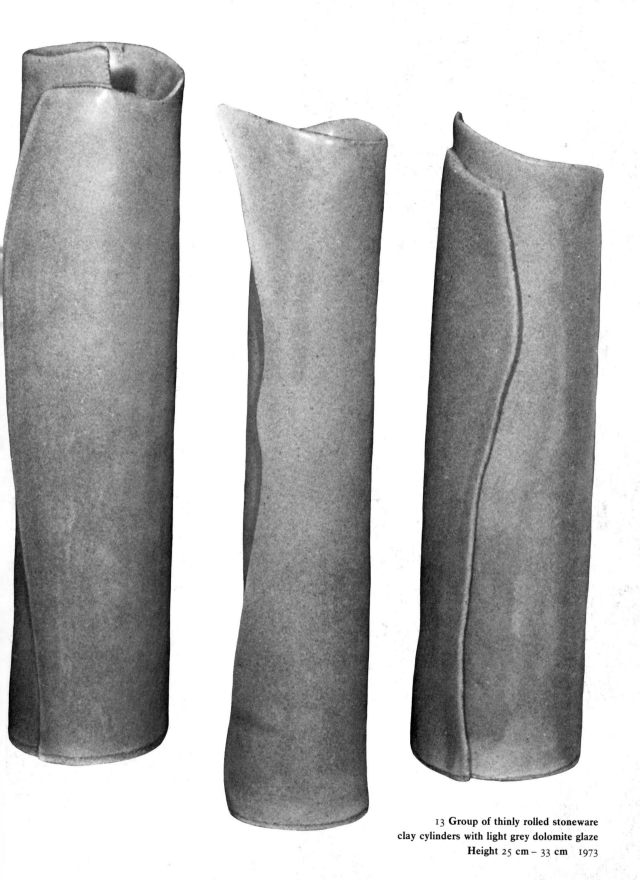

13 **Group of thinly rolled stoneware clay cylinders with light grey dolomite glaze**
Height 25 cm – 33 cm 1973

Hollow pinched unglazed stoneware
rds with iron added to Crammix stoneware body and incised patterns
eight 5 cm – 12 cm   1972

16 Stoneware, pipe clay body
with high iron content, wheel
thrown, paddled and textured.
The dark clay body breaks
through the thinly applied
white dolomite glaze
Height 10 cm – 20 cm   1972

Stoneware with double-glazed
am colour breaking through
blue-green. Incised and
plied design
ight 18 cm   1972

THELMA MARCUSON

17 Thrown and flattened stoneware with base added. Textured surface with manganese wash under light brown matt glaze
Height 30 cm 1972
Coll. L. Goodman

18 Stoneware with black and white dolomite glaze
Diam. 27 cm 1971

19 **Group of three small pinched stoneware forms, the white glaze tinged with blue**
Height 5 cm – 12 cm 1971
Coll. J. C. Cohen

20 **Porcelain with shadowy blue and grey markings under a clear glaze**
Height 8 cm 1973
Coll. Prof. M. Millner

1 'Eendracht maak maght', unglazed ceramic
stoneware sculpture with oxide treatment
Height 18 cm   1973/4
Coll. T. Morris

TIM MORRIS

TO TIM MORRIS output is important. He does not subscribe to the aggrandisement of pottery as an expensive elitist art form.

'Provided a potter puts in a full day's work, pottery is one art form that can be made available to all at reasonable cost,' he insists. He works fast, throwing as much as half a ton of clay a day.

Morris, born in March 1941, trained initially as a painter. At school he showed such flair that he wrote his 'A' levels on the subject two years before he wrote his 'O' levels. Graduating to the St Martin School of Art in London, he swiftly obtained the national diploma in design, majoring in painting. Following this he qualified for the teacher's training diploma at London University. Then he moved to the Central School of Art where he studied pottery under many of Britain's acknowledged masters; Ruth Duckworth (with whom he also worked for a short time), Ian Auld, Kenneth Clark, Dan Arbeid, Gordon Baldwin and John Colbeck.

In 1965 the offer of the use of the family seaside cottage at the Cape, and his own urgent need for a change of scene, brought him to South Africa. For a while he continued with his portraiture while exploring the possibility of starting a pottery studio and workshop.

He later met Helen Martin (Dunstan) and the two decided, somewhat spontaneously, to establish a studio together. The undercapitalised project got under way in the Orchards suburb of Johannesburg with the backing of a group of hopeful students – and some inventive improvisation.

The partnership lasted two years.

In 1967 Morris moved to the farm of furniture

TIM MORRIS

designer John Tabrahams. At Larsens Farm, some miles from Johannesburg, he installed himself in the servants' quarters and his studio in the cow-shed. With the aid of a technical man from a large oil company he built an oil kiln. By now his work was beginning to attract attention, was building up what he terms his 'audience'.

Helen de Leeuw recognised Morris' latent potential and offered him his first one-man exhibition at her Johannesburg gallery. In 1969 this was followed by a one-man exhibition at Lynda Goodman's Gallery which marked a turning-point in his career. It finally affirmed his decision to remain in this medium for which he had developed so much affection. He acquired land near to his existing studio and began to build his rambling, white, steep-pitched studio-home with the aid of two Africans and a patient wife.

The studio itself is simple, spacious and effective. It consists of five sunny rooms housing the clay processing, showroom, kiln room, throwing room and working areas. The 5m³ (175 cubic foot) kiln is separate, set unobtrusively into the main building. Morris fires once every three weeks as a rule, but this can peak up to weekly firings.

Two Africans assist with the clay processing and slabbing, kiln packing and other manual activities. Most of his output is produced on a custom-built electric wheel which is set very low to allow him to pull large pots. Apart from slabbing, he does virtually no hand building except when working on sculptures.

He fires twice, keeps glazing down to basics. Decoration with three high-clay 'house' glazes and a few oxides (iron, cobalt-rutile) is used with a sense of economy. Morris is particularly adept at this, having trained as a painter. His decorative motifs are drawn from nature: stylised butterflies, birds, flowers and plants, which are created with a few careful sweeps of the brush. Most pots are only partially glazed, showing expanses of the clay body. He is at his best working out partnerships of body, form and oxides, as can be seen in several of his sculptural works. His inspiration is rather multi-faceted; a prismic convergence that draws light from both traditional and contemporary pottery, from nature, from society and, to be fair, from the demands of his 'audience'.

2. 'Ducks in Flight', three stoneware vases with iron oxide decoration on a feldspathic glaze Height 77 cm, 51 cm, 46 cm 1974

3 Stoneware with a clay, dolomite and feldspathic glaze, iron slip and cobalt pigment Area of tile 41 cm² 1974

4 Stoneware, thrown and reshaped with applied fins, glazed inside and with sgraffito design over rubbed oxide on outside
Height 15 cm, 21 cm   1971
Coll. G. Clark

5 Group of unglazed thrown stoneware cylindrical jars with oxide design
Height 7 cm – 16 cm   1973
Coll. T. Morris

6 Thrown and hand
built stoneware
'fish-pot' series.
Unglazed and textured
with sgraffito and
oxide design
Height 70 cm – 92 cm
1974

Although interested in traditional pottery, he was indelibly impressed by Middle Eastern pottery during his work on Kathleen Kenyon's dig in Israel, which was close to the Jerusalem Museum. This museum houses one of the most complete collections of early mid-eastern pottery and clay vessels, dating back to the pre-pottery neolithic period of Jericho. The realisation that exceptional pottery was created without glaze millenia ago has undoubtedly had a profound influence on Tim Morris.

Because there are no other strong polarisations in his work, Morris remains highly experimental. A review of his output over the years shows a wide range of designs, not all following a natural evolutionary path. But then he is not in search of the ultimate form of expression.

Tim Morris sums up his own work ethic as follows: 'I think that the traditional potter has tended to assume that there is a norm in pottery, an "absolute truth" that must be reached. Today the potter must reflect the times in which he lives and, whether rightly or wrongly, ours is a period of rapid transition with very temporal values. This constant ebb and flow of mores and attitudes cannot be reflected in a stagnant form, albeit near-perfect.'

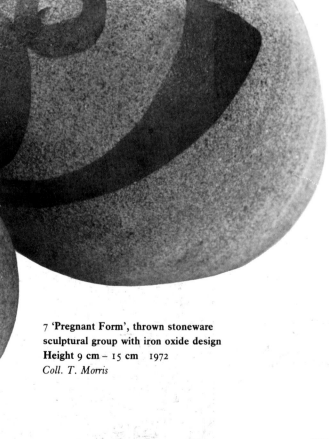

7 'Pregnant Form', thrown stoneware sculptural group with iron oxide design
Height 9 cm – 15 cm 1972
Coll. T. Morris

125

8 'Ceremonial Totem Figures'
Unglazed slabbed stoneware with incised design
Height 17 cm – 38 cm   1973
Coll. T. Morris

TIM MORRIS

9 'Totem' pot. Slab-built textured stoneware
pot with brown glazed neck
Height 18 cm   1973
Coll. T. Morris

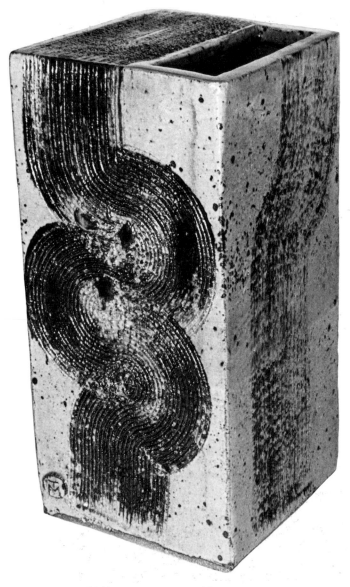

10 Slabbed stoneware pot with
oxide over textured design and
semi-transparent glaze
Height 32 cm 1971

11 'Landscape "Moonside" ', slabbed stoneware
pot with oxide rubbed into the body
Height 30 cm 1970
Coll. T. Morris

12 **Stoneware casseroles, soup bowl, ladle and oil bottle**
Diam. of casseroles 15 cm – 46 cm   1974

13 'Model for sculpture of immense
proportions', hollow slabbed
stoneware ceramic sculpture in
two pieces with black oxide line
Height 20 cm   1971
Coll. T. Morris

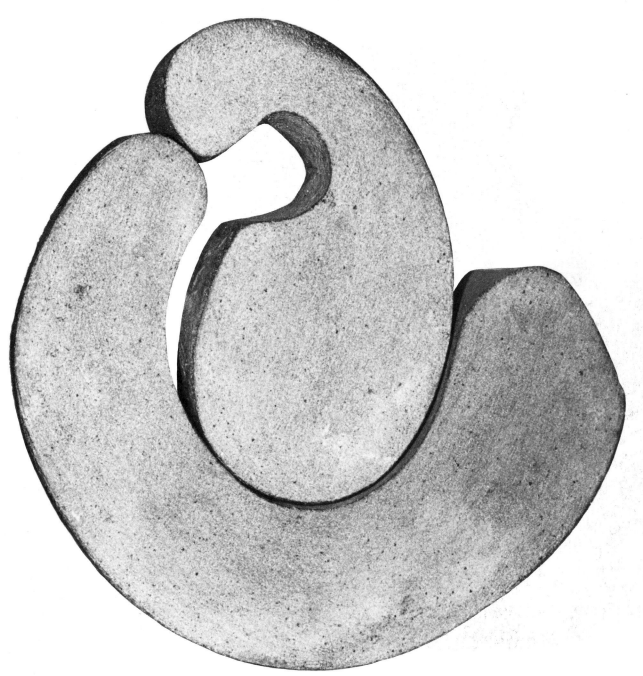

14 'Foetus in Pelvis', unglazed slabbed
stoneware interlocking sculpture
Height 80 cm 1972
Coll. T. Morris

HYM RABINOWITZ

HYM RABINOWITZ works at Eagle's Nest in Constantia, Cape Town. His workshop, situated high on the mountain slopes, has a grand view over the Constantia valley to the surrounding mountains; a view conducive to harmonious and peaceful working conditions.

To Rabinowitz pottery is primarily a craft, with a possible element of art, depending on the form of the pot. Simplicity is the keynote of his shapes and decorations. He produces mainly functional pieces and is a firm believer in the need for repetitive throwing as a basis for creative work.

Hym Rabinowitz was born in Concordia in Namaqualand in 1920. He had his schooling in Port Nolloth and Cape Town, finally qualifying as a chartered accountant. His interest in pottery grew steadily until in 1962 he turned to this craft full-time.

In 1956 he spent six months with Kenneth Quick at the Tregenna Hill Pottery where Quick was turning out oxidised stoneware. In 1961 he worked at White River where Esias Bosch had just established his new workship and was making reduced stoneware in a wood-fired kiln. A visit to the United Kingdom during 1966 and 1967 brought him the opportunity to work with Michael Cardew at Wenford Bridge.

Hym Rabinowitz enjoys travelling, particularly to those areas in Africa he has not yet seen. West African pots impress him especially and he considers them the best made in Africa.

Initially Rabinowitz built a Cardew wood kiln and fired in this for several years. Circumstances later forced a change to oil-firing and the present kiln is a 5,097m^3 (180 cubic foot) square structure with a shallow dome. Four burners ensure satisfactory reduced firings. A nearby pipe clay deposit provides a suitable stoneware body with the addition of feldspar. Pots are bisque-fired before glazing. Four main feldspathic glazes are in use and one of ash and red clay.

White semi-matt feldspathic glazed stoneware wine
bottle with brushed-on iron oxide pigment decoration
Height 30 cm   1973

2 Stoneware dish with oatmeal-
coloured feldspathic glaze
containing 1% iron oxide and a thin
dipped tenmoku glaze on the rim. The feldspathic
tenmoku glaze contains 8% iron oxide
Length 57 cm   1974

3 Stoneware baking dish glazed on the
inside only with a white feldspathic glaze.
Decoration in iron oxide pigment
Length 28 cm   1974

4 **Oatmeal-coloured glazed stoneware dish with wax
decoration, dipped in a thin tenmoku glaze**
Diam. 50 cm 1974

HYM RABINOWITZ

5 **Stoneware with white semi-matt feldspathic glaze**
Height approx. 18 cm 1973

6 Stoneware casserole with feldspathic glaze containing
1% iron oxide which gives an opaque type of celadon. Wax
decoration with iron oxide pigment brushed on top
Width 28 cm 1974

7 Stoneware vase glazed on the inside only with
a tenmoku glaze. Fly ash from the wood-firing gives
a thin glazed texture to the outside surface
Height 17 cm   1962

8 White semi-matt feldspathic glazed stoneware soup
tureen with brushwork decoration in iron oxide pigment
Height 26 cm   1974

HYM RABINOWITZ

9 The jug has a tenmoku glaze under an ash glaze. The ash glaze consists of 75% red clay partly calcined and 25% ash, showing up red under oxidation
Height 12 cm   1969

10 Stoneware ovenware with oatmeal-coloured
feldspathic glaze followed by a thin dip of
tenmoku glaze on rim
Square dish 28 cm² 1974

11 **Oatmeal-coloured feldspathic glazed
stoneware with leaf pattern and
rim in tenmoku glaze**
Diam. 40 cm   1972
Coll. T. Maggs

12 **White semi-matt feldspathic
glazed stoneware bowl**
Diam. 15 cm   1973

13 Stoneware bowl with dark
oatmeal-coloured glaze containing
1½% iron oxide in a feldspathic
glaze. The rim is double-dipped in
a tenmoku glaze
Diam. 16 cm   1974

14 Stoneware covered jar with feldspathic glaze containing 1% iron
oxide which gives an opaque type
of celadon. Decoration is in wax
brushwork with iron oxide pigment
brushed on top
Height 15 cm   1974

15 Stoneware oven-pot glazed on the
inside only with oatmeal-coloured glaze
Height 15 cm   1974

RORKE'S DRIFT

EIGHT AFRICAN POTTERS, working in an open corrugated iron worshop at Rorke's Drift in KwaZulu, produce the only contemporary African pottery in the Republic. It is pleasingly ironical that this harmonious marriage of tribal culture and Western technology should be taking place on a site where, in the last century, the two ideologies clashed on an historical battlefield.

The pottery is part of the Arts and Crafts Centre founded in 1962 by the Evangelical Lutheran Church. Otto Lundbohm is principal of the art school and his wife Malin is manager of the workshops, employing close on 200 local people. Best-known of their activities is the weaving section. The tapestries which are produced have achieved world renown.

Pottery was a late and uneconomical starter, subsidised and supported by the success of the weavers for some time. It was developed from the traditional pot coiling of the local African women, by a Dane, Peter Tyberg, who took the pottery off to a start in 1968. A poor kiln, coupled with unstable local clay, produced very erratic results and a low output. Potters were obliged to keep to sgraffito and oxide slip designs.

In 1971 Marietjie van der Merwe agreed to assist the Centre and began to pay regular visits. Unglazed stoneware had until then been fired in a drip-feed oil kiln. Her first task was to improve the quality of the clay and repair the kiln so that it could reach a higher temperature and achieve a more even heat distribution. The new 4,247m³ (150 cubic foot) kiln, designed by her and built under her supervision, was completed in March 1973 and fires on paraffin through six drip-feed burners. She also turned her attention to producing a neutral, quiet kaolin matt glaze (based on a Cardew recipe: 33% feldspar, 22% whiting, 35% kaolin and 10% silica) that would enhance the slip decoration. The slips that are now in use with this glaze are a black slip (a combination

1 Hand built stoneware by Dinah Molefe
with iron and black slips under a
heavily reduced kaolin matt glaze
Height 27 cm   1973
Coll. M. Lundbohm

2 Dinah Molefe painting a hand bu
'ikamba' shape with a s▸

19

3 Hand built stoneware by Miriam
Khumalo with applied clay and painted
decoration in iron and black slips
under a kaolin matt glaze
Height 14 cm   1974

4 A collection of hand built stoneware
pots by the Molefe women with painted
and scratched decorations under a slip
glaze. The early pots had a shiny
lacquer-like finish to the glaze
Early 1972

of 4% cobalt, 4% manganese and 6% iron), an iron slip, a yellow ochre slip and an umber slip which, like the yellow ochre slip, is a half and half mixture with stoneware clay.

Now fully viable, plans are afoot for expansion of the pottery, aided by a grant from the Anglo-American Corporation. The new workshop will be able to house 30 potters.

The present team is headed by Gordon Mbatha, who joined the Centre as a weaver in 1965 and was the first man to join what had been until 1968 an all-women section. A potter in his own right, he is also the group's 'foreman' and responsible for all glazing and firing. With him work another two male throwers – Ephraim Ziqubu and Joel Sibisi.

The men who shape their pots on the wheel rely mainly on the decoration to give the pots their specific character. Much more time is spent on the decorations, which are lavishly applied, than on the forming of the pots. This may have developed because of the lack of plasticity of the earlier stoneware they used and perhaps also because the huge concrete kick wheels were more difficult to control.

The women do not work on the wheel, remaining within the confines of a pot coiling tradition that goes back centuries. Before working at Rorke's Drift the women were already experienced pot coilers, making the traditional 'ikamba' (beer pots) for their households. These were usually decorated with simple sgraffito designs, then fired in an open dung fire and blackened through reduction and smoke. These porous pots are ideal for storing liquids and keeping

6 Hand built stoneware by Lephina Molefe with applied clay and painted decoration in black slip under a kaolin matt glaze
Height 51 cm   1973

7 Hand built stoneware by Dinah Molefe with applied clay and painted design in black slip under a kaolin matt glaze
Height 24 cm   1972

5 Hand built stoneware by Dinah Molefe with black slip design under a kaolin matt glaze
Height 17 cm   1973

8 Seated, Gordon Mbatha with from left
to right, Ephraim Ziqubu and Joel Sibisi

them cool. Although they now work in stoneware these potters are merely continuing where their traditions left off and the shapes are easily identifiable.

The senior of these potters and one of the leading women potters in the country is Dinah Molefe. With her work her daughter Loviniah, two relatives, Lephina and Ivy, and Miriam Khumalo. All the potters are Zulu except for the four Molefe women who are Basotho.

Like the weavers, the potters work as independent artists and are left entirely free to develop as individuals. There is, of course, an inevitable sameness of shape and decoration. Working in isolation in a small creative community and drawing inspiration from common traditional roots is bound to produce an apparently uniform style. But it is deceptive, for the individualism of each potter's work soon manifests itself. The tribal social inhibitions have a noticeable effect and the men are more adventurous in their design work which is detailed and often narrative. The women do not stray far from the geometric patterns with which they are familiar or from the Zulu and Basuto custom of applied design and sgraffito.

Work by these potters is unique in its social significance and design. It is also an experiment which is unlikely to be repeated with the same simplicity and honesty.

9 Thrown stoneware by Joel Sibisi with sgraffito decoration over umber slip and glazed on the inside only
Height 35 cm 1973

10 Stoneware by Joel Sibisi, glazed inside, with a representational design in black oxide against light stoneware body
Height 31 cm
Coll. G. Clark

11 Unstacking the 4,247m³ (150 cu.ft) kiln
built in March 1973

13 Thrown stoneware b
Ephraim Ziqubu with blac
slip painted under
kaolin matt gla
Height 18 cm 19

12 Two thrown stoneware pots by Joel Sibisi with iron and
umber slip and sgraffito decoration, glazed on inside
only with an iron glaze
Height 36 cm, 25 cm 1974

15 Thrown stoneware by Ephraim Ziqubu
with iron slip and
sgraffito decoration, glazed
inside only with an iron
glaze
Height 34 cm   1974

14 Three thrown stoneware jugs by
Ephraim Ziqubu with
applied decoration and black slip
painted under a kaolin matt glaze
Height 22 cm, 24 cm, 22 cm
1974

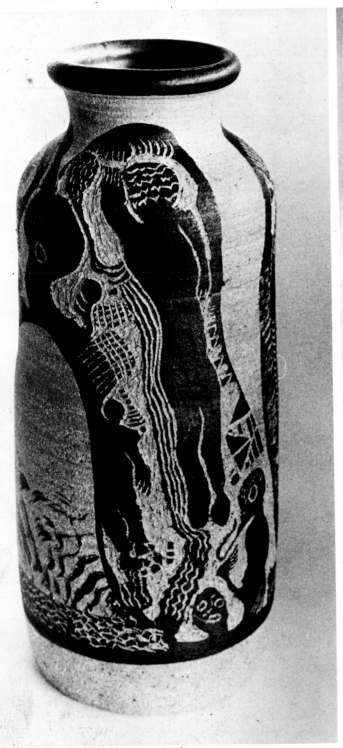

16 Thrown stoneware by Gordon Mbatha with umber slip and sgraffito decoration. Glazed on inside only with an iron glaze and fired to 1 300° C. Decoration shows the preacher Shembe when he made his unsuccessful attempt to fly to prove God's faith in him
Height 37 cm 1974

17 'The time when the animals and people were mixed.' Thrown stoneware pot by Gordon Mbatha with umber slip and sgraffito design, glazed on the inside only
Height 49 cm 1973
Coll. M. van der Merwe

18 Thrown stoneware bowl by
Gordon Mbatha, slip painted
without glaze and fired
to approx. 1 200° C
Diam. 23 cm 1971
Coll. E. L. C. Art and Craft Centre, Rorke's Drift

19 **Hand built stoneware by Dinah and Loviniah Molefe**
(the largest one is by Loviniah), scratched, sculptured
and painted under a kaolin matt glaze
1973

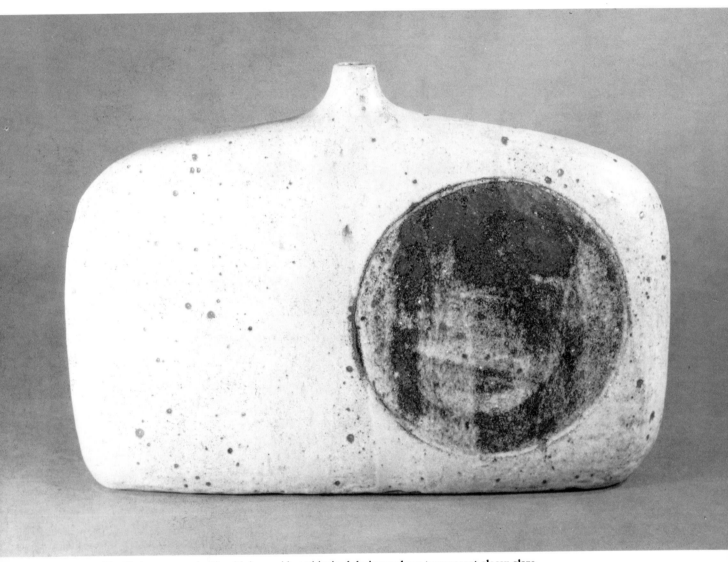

1 **Moulded stoneware bottle with iron oxide and incised design under a transparent glossy glaze**
Height 25 cm
Coll. G. Clark

THABA BOSIGO

THABA BOSIGO (Mountain of the Night) pottery is something of a craft miracle. Two years ago, in 1972, when Peter Hayes was brought out by the Lesotho National Development Corporation, he had a deserted brewery as his studio and no trained potters.

One of the first jobs was to build a clay plant. Hayes himself constructed a blunger and pugmill and acquired a compressor and filter-press. With the clay plant working, shelving and benches installed together with four Podmore electric wheels, two Ferro-Enamel wheels and three Bernard Leach kick wheels, he began employing some would-be potters.

Peter Hayes threw the first pot, a simple cylinder, to the utter bewilderment of his onlookers. Then his trainees, armed with balls of clay and a potter's wheel, set about their task with the usual antics of people on the wheel for the first time. If nothing else, they were enjoying themselves. At the same time women were being trained to coil and slab. Weeks of training passed, each step being taken with great care, yet most of the first efforts had to be returned to the clay bin.

By this time thoughts were turning to the urgent need for a kiln. It was decided to build a small 0,765m³ (27 cubic foot) oil-fired down-draught kiln outside the studio. This permitted the testing of glazes and the firing of those pots which now merited it. The first firing took place on a cold clear night with Peter Hayes watching the pyrometric cones slowly bending, surrounded by the shadowy mountains of Lesotho.

PETER HAYES

THABA BOSIGO

Since then Peter Hayes has built up a studio with a complement of 28 people producing individually hand-made pottery, with the help of two giant Dave Berry kilns. Mostly, reduction firing is done outside in the oil-fired kiln, but on occasions when the elements in the Dave Berry electric kilns are about to be replaced, reduction firing is achieved by using moth-balls to create a reduction atmosphere.

Hayes has developed interesting glazes of which the metallic petalite, an attractive ash and a crackle glaze are the most pleasing. A succesful design experiment was the 'Letima' pots (Fig. 3), which were derived from the style of decorating the exterior of the Basotho huts when the young women become eligible for marriage. The women, from time to time, produce interesting and unusual original pieces, such as the pot illustrated in Fig. 9.

Peter Hayes, born in 1946, is a quietly spoken ceramic sculptor who studied in Birmingham. After a short career in commercial art, he and his wife did a virtual 'moonlight flit' from the advertising world in London to St Mawes, a small fishing village on the Cornish coast, where they set up a studio. An inclusion in the County Workshop directory brought Hayes a letter from the Lesotho National Development Corporation's Wynaand van Graan and the beginning of his adventure in Southern Africa.

The output at Thaba Bosigo places highly decorative pottery within the reach of all. It is also an interesting study in craft economics, showing the craft talent and potential which lies largely untapped in Southern Africa.

2 Coiled stoneware pot with thrown
neck, the finger marks made in
joining each coil giving texture.
Matt white glaze fired in oxidation to 1 250° C
Height 75 cm   1973

3 Coiled stoneware 'Letima' pot with throw
neck and design carved with a sharp to
when the pot was dry. A band of whit
matt glaze was applied by brush afte
bisque-firing and then rubbed off leavi
the incised carving filled with glaz
Reduction fired to 1 285°
Height 45 cm   19

5 Slabbed stoneware
pots with thrown necks,
white matt glaze and
cobalt oxide design
Height 15 cm   1973

6 Stoneware with brown
semi-transparent glaze
and iron oxide design
Height 10 cm   1973

Stoneware. Black and white engobe with sgraffito
sign under a transparent glaze
eight 37 cm   1973

7 Slabbed stoneware with thrown top
and semi-transparent brown glaze
with iron oxide design
Height 35 cm   1973

8 Thrown stoneware 'pear' pot dipped
in a fairly thick stable petalite transparent
green glaze over a wax resist design and
fired to 1 285° **C** producing a crackle finish
Height 40 cm   1974

THABA BOSIGO

9 Simple stoneware slab pot with thrown
neck, made by one of the women workers.
Wax resist technique has been used and
the pot fired to 1 285° C
Height 15 cm   1972

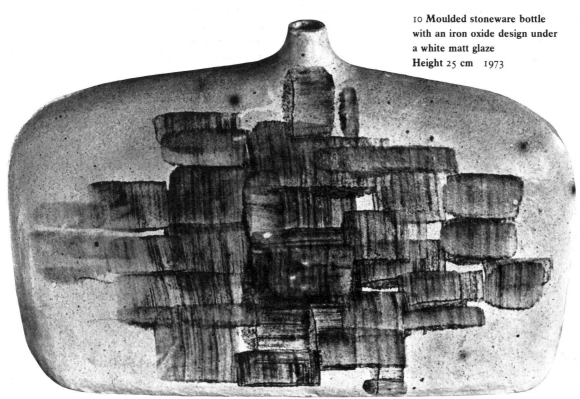

10 Moulded stoneware bottle
with an iron oxide design under
a white matt glaze
Height 25 cm   1973

11 Porous pot made from
common brick clay by
Peter Hayes. Ten percent coal
is added to the body, this burns
out during the firing leaving
ash deposits on the surface.
Fired to 1 000° C
Height 38 cm

12 Stoneware slabbed pots with thrown necks and applied design under a white matt glaze
Height 25 cm, 35 cm   1973

13 Coiled stoneware with carved design by Peter Hayes. Iron oxide and a white matt glaze were rubbed into the body
Height 28 cm   1972

MARIETJIE VAN DER MERWE

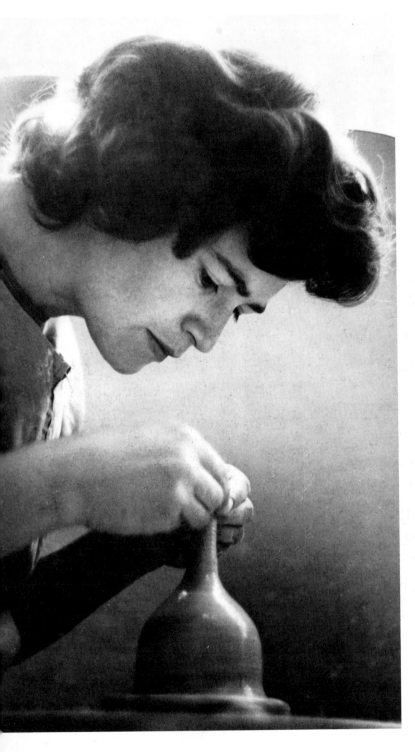

LIKE SO MANY potters, Marietjie van der Merwe did not set out with the direct intention of following this craft. Born in 1935 in Gwelo, Rhodesia, she studied initially as an organist and music teacher at the University of Stellenbosch. In 1957 she moved to Los Angeles with her husband where she studied at the University of California, obtaining first a B.A. and then a M.A. degree, majoring in design.

Towards the end of her studies in the U.S.A., she concentrated on pottery under Laura Andreson, inheriting this gifted teacher's love of bottle shapes with narrow necks or round bulbous forms. While in America, she was also able to experiment with porcelain.

In 1963 she returned to South Africa, settling in Grahamstown. Using an electric kiln, she worked in a dark red semi-stoneware. Her first one-man exhibition was staged in Cape Town in 1966.

The electric kiln proved to be too limiting, so, armed with a copy of Paul Soldner's booklet on kiln construction, she set about building a $0,707m^3$ (25 cubic foot) catenary arch kiln.

After much experimentation and several alterations to the kiln, burners and gas-supply, she was able eventually to reach the temperature of $1\,300°\,C$ necessary for stoneware, but it then became apparent that the firebricks were impregnated with salt glaze which ruined her glazes. After futile attempts to rid the kiln of the effect of these bricks, the entire kiln was pulled down and rebuilt using new bricks. In retrospect, she regrets not having had the insight to use the kiln, if only temporarily, for salt-glazing.

At last, after a year of disappointments, frustrations and lost pots, the kiln finally worked. However, the day of her first successful firing was also the date on which her husband accepted a new post in Cape Town. Three months later they moved.

In Cape Town another kiln was built, this time firing with oil. A long period of experimentation with oil-pumps, compressors, fans and burners followed before the kiln worked to her satisfaction.

1 Porcelain tea-pot with an opaque feldspathic glaze containing
4% iron giving an orange-yellow colour. Reduction fired to 1 300° C
Width 15 cm   1963

MARIETJIE VAN DER MERWE

In 1969, accompanying her husband to the
U.S.A. for a sabbatical year, she studied at the
Chicago Art Institute, and experimented with
lustres, porcelain and raku.

Since her return she has concentrated on a basic
barium matt glaze, in which she varies the colour by
the addition of copper or rutile, or cobalt slips
under the glaze. Another favourite is a magnesium
matt glaze. Occasional use is made of celadon, tenmoku and crystalline glazes.

Since 1971 she has become closely associated with
Rorke's Drift and is their visiting teacher in pottery.
Marietjie van der Merwe's work has recently been
influenced by the coiled pottery of the Basotho
women at Rorke's Drift. Most particularly, this has
come from the elderly and dignified Dinah Molefe,
who gently coils the most simple traditional forms.

Marietjie van der Merwe has to some degree put
back into pottery as much as she has taken from it.
Apart from the work at Rorke's Drift, she has also
written a chapter on pottery for an Afrikaans series
of books and teaches part-time at the Frank Joubert
Art Centre at Newlands, where pottery is taught as
a high school subject.

Approachable and helpful, she has encouraged
many amateur potters, regretting that the fragmen-
tation of her time has restricted her development
and the quantity of her output.

'What I am longing for is to make pots while in a
state of "no-mindedness", which Soetzu Yanagi, the
Japanese craft-philosopher, sees as essential for the
creation of beauty. This I believe is only possible
while maintaining a steady and repetitive production
of similar kinds of shapes and unexpectedly finding
a pot emerging with that quality of life that gives
meaning to being a potter. Such a pot can encourage
and inspire further work.'

2 **Left: Coiled stoneware vase with a matt barium glaze
poured over a dolomite glaze and reduction fired to 1 300° C
Height 37 cm 1974**

3 **Centre: Porcelain slab vase with torn rim, reduction
fired to 1 300° C with a clear feldspathic glaze and then fired
with a film of copper lustre to 700° C
Height 26 cm 1970**
Coll. M. van der Merwe

4 **Right: Stoneware vase with dolomite glaze reduction
fired to 1 300° C
Height 19 cm 1973**
Coll. C. Theron

5 **Partially glazed stoneware composite form reduction fired to** I 300° **C**
Height 16 **cm**   1962
Coll. M. Plaut

6 Porcelain bowl with crystalline glaze containing copper. The basic
colour is white with the palest blue-green. Reduction fired to 1 300° C
Diam. 15 cm   1963   *Coll. of the Art Dept, University of California, Los Angeles*

7 Stoneware casserole with a reduction fired magnesium
glaze. Spots are caused where iron in the clay was drawn
through the glaze by the reducing action of the fire
Diam. 24 cm   1962   *Coll. M. van der Merwe*

8 Porcelain vase with iron in the feldspathic
glaze, reduction fired to I 300° C
Height 16 cm 1963
Coll. W. E. G. Louw

9 Porcelain vase with crystalline glaze containing cobalt
and iron, reduction fired to I 300° C
Width 14 cm 1963
Coll. of the Art Dept, University of California, Los Angeles

10 **Thrown stoneware vases reduction fired with a matt barium glaze. From left to right: iron and rutile sprayed over the glaze; 4% copper carbonate in the glaze; and on the far right, a cobalt slip under the glaze with a spray of iron over the glaze Height** 39 cm, 47 cm, 31 cm, 38 cm 1973/4

11 **Three stoneware vases with a tenmoku glaze
reduction fired to** 1 300° **C
Height** 16 cm, 14 cm, 22 cm   1974

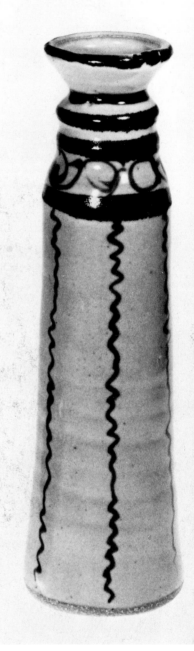

12 Stoneware vase with
a black tenmoku glaze reduction
fired to 1 300° C
Height 20 cm   1973
Coll. E. Plaut

13 Small stoneware jug with fat magnesium glaze over
cobalt slip and decorated with iron pigment.
Vase decorated with iron and cobalt pigments
Height 10 cm, 24 cm   1974

MARIETJIE VAN DER MERWE

14 Three stoneware jugs. The two on the left
have a barium matt glaze sprayed over with iron
oxide, and the one on the right a feldspathic
semi-opaque glaze over a cobalt slip and brushed
with iron oxide
Height 26 cm, 30 cm, 25 cm   1974

15 **Large coiled stoneware form with a barium matt
glaze sprayed with iron oxide. Reduction fired to** 1 300° C
Height 40 cm   1973

HANNATJIE VAN DER WAT

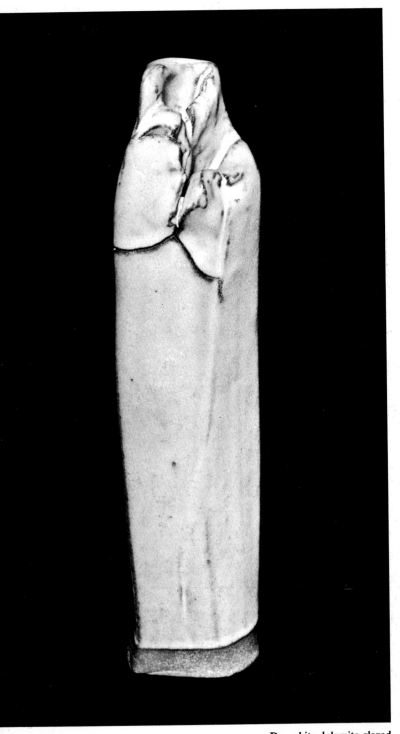

1 **Dry white dolomite glazed**
stoneware sculptural piece
hand built from a solid block and
fired to 1 280° C
Height 20 cm

HANNATJIE VAN DER WAT (née Schabort) was born in Frankfort, Orange Free State, in 1923. She obtained the national art teacher's certificate in 1944 at Witwatersrand Technical Art School where she gained experience in clay modelling. Her tutor, Maurice van Essche, influenced her to major in painting, however.

After leaving art school she taught at Transvaal high schools for a while until she married and became absorbed in her home and bringing up her three children.

Hannatjie van der Wat's professional career in painting dates from her renewed studies in 1962 with Sidney Goldblatt.

She participated in all significant group shows in the country. Her paintings at this stage were abstract and artistically conventional, later becoming more colourful and formal, leading to precise hard-edge compositions.

Experiment with ceramics began in 1972 through a friendship with the potter Helen Martin (Dunstan) who invited her to her studio school to 'play with clay'. Hannatjie van der Wat took up the invitation with scepticism, not expecting to return more than once or twice at most. But from the moment that she began handling the clay, a creative empathy began to take hold of her. By her second visit, a very clear direction had emerged. It was a contradiction of all the rules of pottery – solid heavy slabs of clay twisted and pressured into forms.

Credit must go to Helen Dunstan, too. Herself a disciplined and well-trained potter, she disregarded her instincts and made no attempt to influence the work that began to flow. In fact she became Hannatjie van der Wat's guardian, isolating her from any distractions. The first 'outsider' to see the work was Ferdinand Haenggi who offered her an exhibition. This was held in October 1973 at Gallery 21, Johannesburg.

Said art critic Richard Cheales: 'Down the years this artist has sought simplicity in her modern paintings. In this unusual show, using clay as her material

(instead of paint), she achieves shapes of such utter simplicity that they would be stark were it not for the underlying impression of subtle sensitivity.'

Hannatjie van der Wat does not refer to herself as a potter and sees her work rather as the product of a sculptor.

Her technique is simple. First the clay is very thoroughly wedged so that the heavy slabs and tubes will survive the firing. Having produced a satisfying basic shape, the moment of creation comes quickly. A gentle but firm twist of the clay, the pressure of the palms creating contours, and the work is complete.

What makes the work valid is that it is not the first accidental achievement of an amateur potter.

'From the first moment until the last, several months later, there was never any alteration in the theme in which I was working, because I found such clarity in what I was doing,' she says.

Since her exhibition in October 1973, Hannatjie van der Wat has continued in this style, almost intuitively shaping her forms. While it is difficult to speculate on the direction her work will now take, there is no doubt that it will continue to be exciting and relevant.

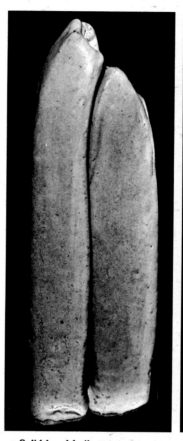

3 Solid hand built stoneware interlocking pieces. Dry white dolomite glaze burnished with red iron oxide, the pink colour merging into the turquoise of the glaze stain
Height 24 cm
Coll. H. van der Wat

4 Completely solid hand built stoneware interlocking upright images with dry white dolomite glaze
Height 28 cm

Three solid hand built stoneware pieces with dry white dolomite glaze
Height 14 cm – 30 cm

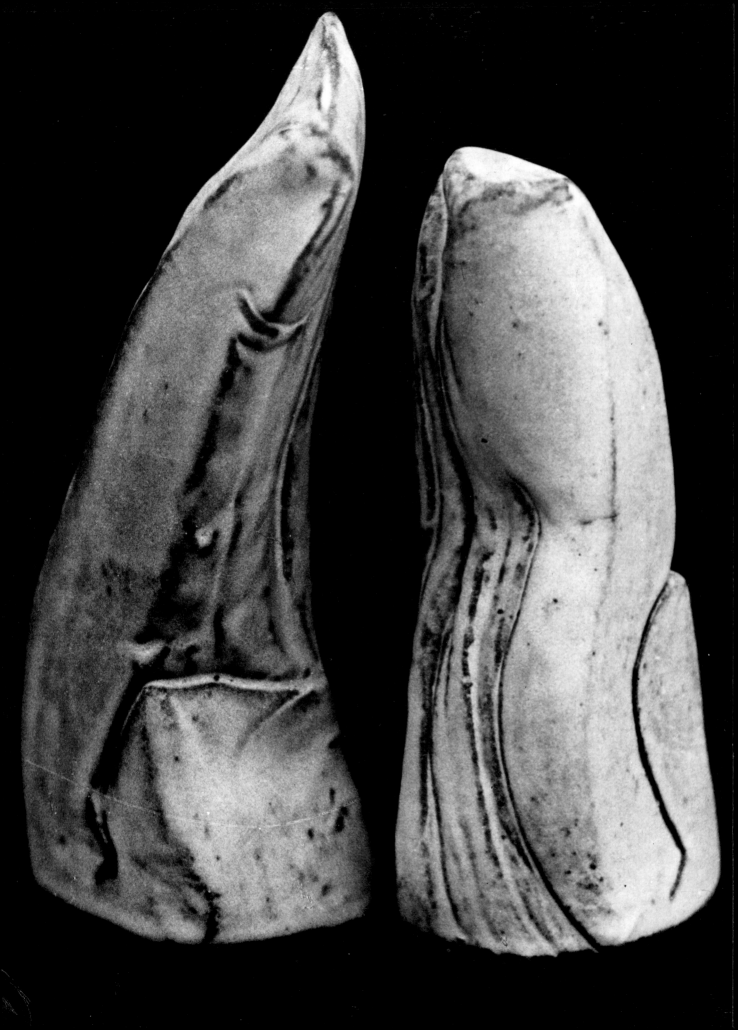

6 **Round hand built stoneware piece pierced
with fingers and cut with a wire.
Greyish-pink dolomite glaze fired to 1 280° C
Height 6 cm, 15 cm**
Coll. H. van der Wat

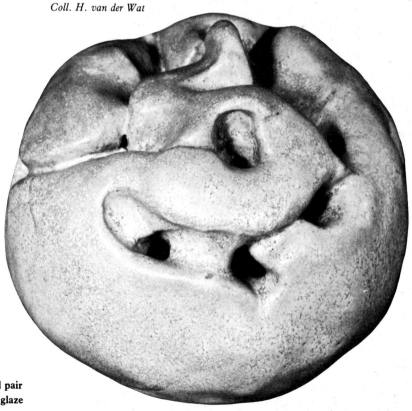

7 **Round-shaped solid
sculptured stoneware piece with
pink dolomite glaze
Height 12 cm**

**Hand built solid
stoneware sculptural pair
with white dolomite glaze
fired to 1 280° C
Height 28 cm, 30 cm**

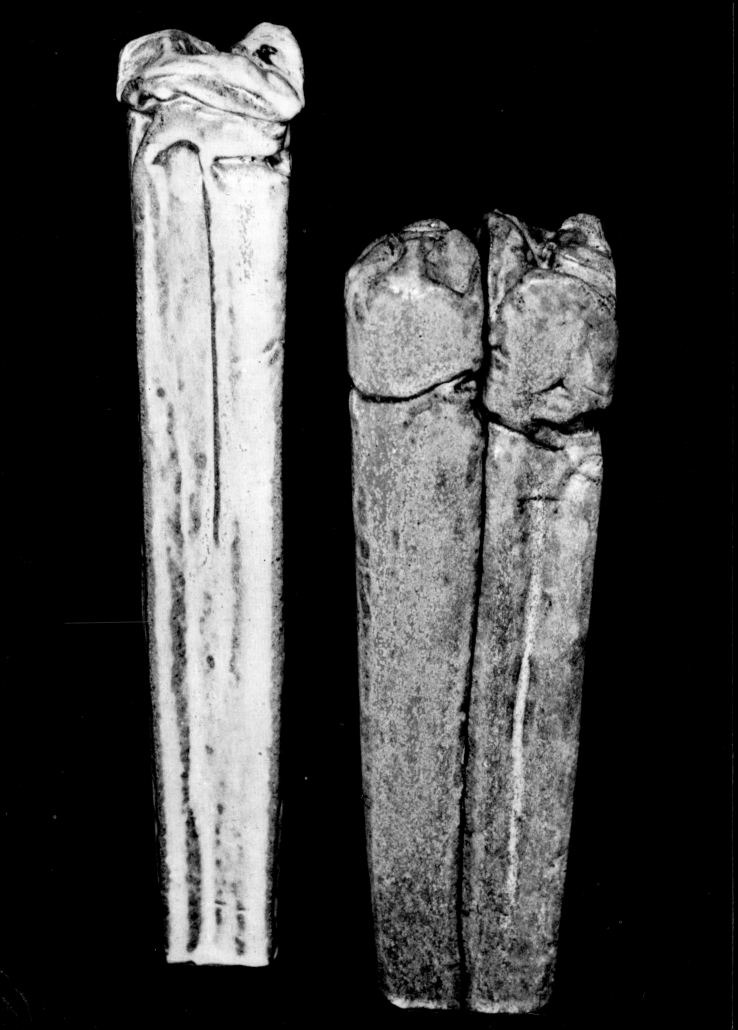

HANNATJIE VAN DER WAT

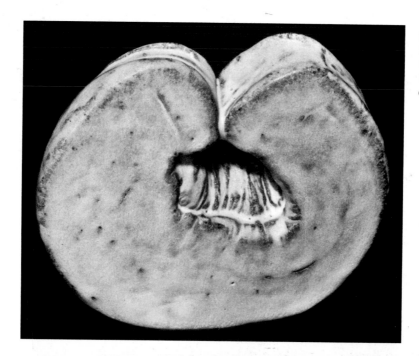

9 Hand built stoneware solid
piece with dry white
dolomite glaze fired to 1 280° C
Width 15 cm
Coll. H. van der Wat

White dolomite glazed
stoneware hand built
from a solid block.
On the right, two uprights
fired into one piece.
The dolomite glaze is
burnished with red iron oxide
and fired to 1 280° C
Height 36 cm, 28 cm

10 Hand built stoneware solid pieces.
Dry white dolomite glaze, burnished
with red iron oxide which adds pink
colour to the glaze, fired to 1 280° C
Height 11 cm – 18 cm

ANDREW WALFORD

ONE OF THE COUNTRY'S few master potters, Andrew Walford draws his strength from his sensitive use of design, colour and his stern, introspective self-discipline which maintains a high standard of work from his studio. The feeling of control which is apparent in all his activity is understandable. More than most, Walford has been fully and widely exposed to an atmosphere of sharp artistic competition. He grew up in a climate of intense striving and creativity. His mother is a painter, now living in Florence; his father, an interior decorator; and his brother, an accomplished furniture designer.

It is not surprising therefore that his interest in pottery began at the early age of ten and has continued unabated since. Walford, who was born on December 4, 1942, admits that his school days were a waste of time apart from the art classes and P.T. He is too much the pragmatist ever to live in peace with drab theory. Even at the Durban Art School this was his problem. Finally he gave up wrestling with history of art and other compulsory 'non-essentials'. After a six month sculpture course, he began an apprenticeship at the Walsh Marais Studio in Durban.

Walford then moved to Johannesburg to continue his training with Sammy Liebermann and he looks back on this experience with warmth. At the age of nineteen, he felt sufficiently confident to open his own studio on a gift of R1 000 from his mother. Initially he built two electric kilns but found them unsatisfactory.

'They were good enough for baking cakes,' he recalls, 'but less than ideal for firing pottery.'

Soon afterwards he built an oil kiln and concentrated on stoneware.

Three years later he closed his studio and migrated to Europe, travelling extensively and meeting leading potters such as Lucie Rie, Bernard Leach and Michael Cardew. During his stay in Scandinavia he

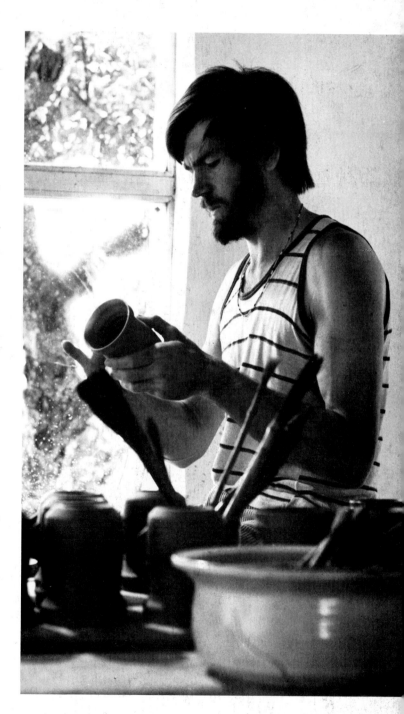

Unglazed porcelain with individually thrown spouts, reduction fired in a saggar in a coal kiln to 1 450° C
Height 23 cm   1966

2 Celadon and tenmoku glazed porcelain
vase wood-fired in a reduction
atmosphere to 1 350° C. The knobs were
extruded and pushed on to the thrown vase
individually, brushed with iron oxide
and then dipped
Height 18 cm   1965

was invited by Stig Lindberg and Lisa Larsen to work at the Gustavberg factory.

From Scandinavia he moved to Germany for what was to prove a not entirely satisfying experience. Investing in a large kiln and studio on the edge of the Black Forest, firing with wood and oil, he soon found himself in trouble with the Staufen bureaucracy. His studio was declared a fire hazard and closed down. Then, too, his opinion of the German potters was not a sympathetic one. He signed a year's contract to teach at the Hamburg Academy of Art, only to find that he and his students had little in common.

His stay in Germany was nonetheless fruitful, giving him the opportunity of becoming acquainted with porcelain, firing in a coal kiln which had not been used for twenty-five years and building up a small yet significant following of German collectors.

In 1967 he returned to South Africa to work in a make-shift studio adjoining his brother's furniture factory. Some time later he moved to his present home at Nshongweni in the Valley of a Thousand Hills, Natal.

In 1969 Walford travelled widely through the Far East, visiting Bombay, Ceylon, Singapore and Bangkok. In Japan he was introduced to Shoji Hamada, a declared living national treasure and one of the greatest potters alive.

Today Walford is totally involved with the Japanese and Korean philosophy of pottery, having 'washed-out' most of the influence of his Scandinavian style although it still appears in his work from time to time. He believes it is good and formative for a potter to have worked through various styles.

'From each involvement something will remain

3 Porcelain bowl fired to
1 450° C in a reduction
atmosphere in a coal kiln.
Sgraffito surface inlaid
with iron, cobalt and
manganese oxides and a
white matt glaze
Diam. 13 cm   1966

4 Porcelain with semi-
transparent glaze,
reduction fired to 1 380° C
Diam. 14 cm   1972

ANDREW WALFORD

that is your own and so one works slowly towards a highly individual indentity.'

Predominant concern in his work is in being true to the medium and imparting as much life as possible to the clay.

'For me a pot looks its best immediately after being thrown or turned. It is still damp and vital. All the other movements, glazing and decorating should preserve this state of aliveness. Though I have made thousands of pots, I always try to make *this* one more alive than the last. Each movement in making the pot has its own rules. On each pot one can see quite clearly by the finger marks, the marks of the turning rod and the decoration, how the potter thinks and feels for his medium. If a pot settles on a table like a butterfly, that is about it!'

Walford fires in a large 4,247m³ (150 cubic foot) oil kiln in a reduction atmosphere to 1 380° C. Except for slab and press-moulding all work is done on a Wally Gilbert wheel, a precision piece of engineering based on a principle which Walford brought back from Germany, combining some of the advantages of both the kick and electric wheel.

Andrew Walford's current concern is with making pots, although he enjoys expressing his ideas in sculpture and tile panels, one of which is in the Killie Campbell Museum in Durban.

5 Unglazed stoneware gourd. Thrown shapes patted and joined when leather-hard. When dry, scoured with steel wool and reduction fired to 1 380° C in oil kiln
Height 12 cm   1970

6 Unglazed stoneware gourd group reduction fired in oil kiln
Height 9 cm - 15 cm   1970

7 Press-moulded porcelain
with thrown neck and iron
and cobalt design under
white semi-transparent
glaze. Reduction fired to
1 380° C in oil-fired kiln
Height 30 cm 1973

8 Press-moulded
stoneware with wax resist
and oxide design
Height 37 cm 1972

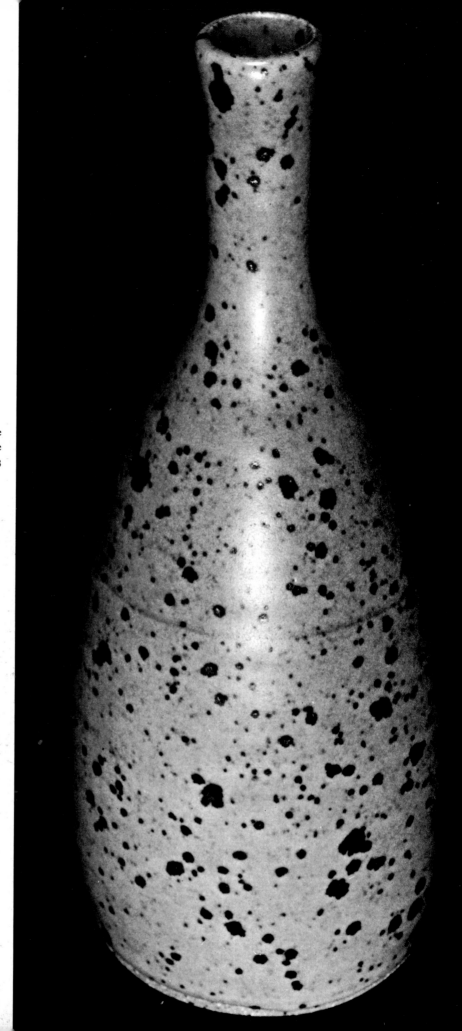

9 Iron-speckled white
semi-matt glazed stoneware
Height 26 cm   1973

ANDREW WALFORD

10 **Off-white transparent crackle-glazed stoneware with iron speckles, reduction fired in oil kiln Height** 13 cm 1971

11 White semi-matt glazed stoneware with iron oxide design. Heavy iron spots in the clay were brought out by the reduction atmosphere. Fired to 1 380° C in oil kiln Height 18 cm 1973

12 Hand thrown porcelain vases with
individually assembled 'nails'. Mutton-fat white
glaze reduced in a coal-fired kiln to 1 450° C
Height 14 cm   1966

13 Porcelain vase dipped in a white glaze
with wax resist decoration and
brushed-on iron oxide. Reduction fired
in oil kiln to 1 380° C
Height 16 cm   1973

14 Stoneware with wax resist and iron
oxide design under white gloss glaze,
reduction fired to 1 380° C in oil kiln
Height 14 cm   1973

15 Stoneware with an iron oxide design
under blue-green semi-matt glaze,
reduction fired to 1 380° C in oil kiln
Height 30 cm   1973

16 Tenmoku glazed stoneware
fired in oil kiln to 1 250° C
Height 15 cm   1963

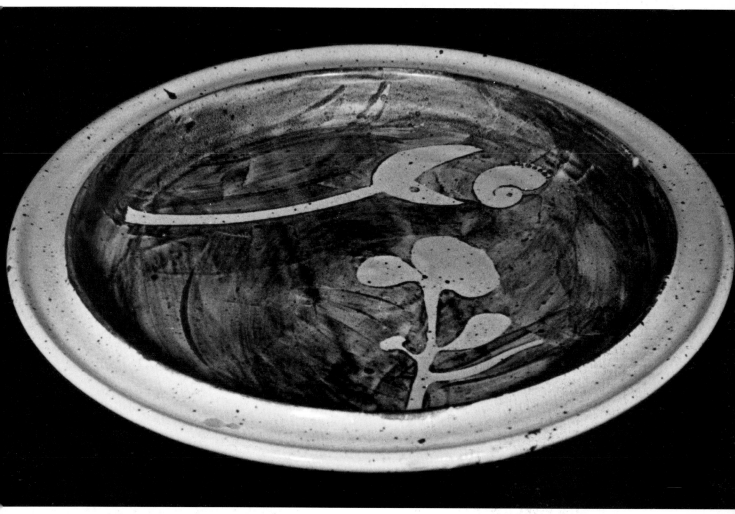

17 **Off-white opaque glazed stoneware platter
decorated with stencils and iron engobe
and reduction fired to** 1 380° C in oil kiln
Diam. 43 cm 1973

GLOSSARY

ASH GLAZE — Glaze in which the ashes of trees, grasses or other plants are used principally as fluxing agents (to promote fusion) for high temperature glazes

BLUNGER — Machine for stirring and mixing ceramic materials, usually the ingredients of the clay body, with water

BODY — Material from which the pot is made. A mixture of clays and non-plastic materials that has suitable malleable and firing properties

CELADON GLAZE — Glaze, originating in China, fired in a reduction atmosphere. The subtle pale grey-green glaze is obtained from a small percentage (usually 1% to 2%) of iron

COILING — A hand building technique. One method of coiling is to use clay which has been rolled into coils and then layering them one on top of the other to create the desired form

CRACKLE GLAZE — Crazing used intentionally as a form of decoration and sometimes emphasised by staining the cracks

CRAWLING — Bare patches where glaze has failed to adhere to the clay, or where the glaze has retracted into drops

CRAZING — A fine network of cracks in the glaze caused by differences in contraction between the body and glaze during cooling, or delayed expansion of the body

CRYSTALLINE GLAZE — Characteristic of these glazes are crystal formations which develop during the slow cooling of the kiln

DOLOMITE — A calcium magnesium carbonate used as a flux in a glaze

EARTHENWARE — A low-fired body which is non-vitreous and opaque. Fired between 1 050°C and 1 180°C

ENGOBE — Another name for a coloured slip

FELDSPATHIC GLAZE — Glazes containing feldspar as the primary flux. Feldspar is the principal flux in stoneware glazes

FILTER-PRESS — Equipment for dewatering clay

FLUX — The ingredient in the glaze which promotes the fusion of the silica by lowering the melting-point

FLY ASH — Ash carried by draught through a kiln and which may be deposited on the ware resulting in a glazed surface

GLAZE — Smooth, glasslike surface layer on the fired clay body. It is applied to the clay body, usually after the initial bisque-firing, and melted on during the glaze firing

GROG — Crushed fired clay of various degrees of fineness added to clay bodies to give strength, reduce shrinkage or provide a textured surface

HAND BUILDING — Technique of building with clay where the wheel is not used

KAOLIN GLAZE — Glaze rich in kaolin giving a typical matt surface

KICK WHEEL — Potter's wheel propelled by a kicking motion of the foot

LEATHER-HARD — The halfway stage between wet and dry clay

MUTTON-FAT GLAZE — Glaze resembling the thick semi-transparent quality of mutton fat

ONCE FIRED — Bisque-firing and glaze-firing combined in one firing

OXIDATION — Fired in a clear atmosphere with a plentiful air-supply

OXIDE — Generally refers to the colouring oxides used to colour clay, slip or glaze. Most commonly used are: iron which gives brown or green; manganese which gives brown or purple; cobalt which gives blue; and copper which gives green

PETALITE — Used as a source of lithia in glazes. A fluxing mineral with a high melting-point

PINCH POTS — Small pots made by depressing and shaping clay with the thumbs and fingers

PORCELAIN — A high-fired vitreous white body with a translucent quality due to its glassy nature. Fired between 1 250°C and 1 400°C

PRESS MOULDING — Forming plastic clay in a plaster mould by pressing it against the mould face

PUGMILL — Mechanical aid in working the clay to achieve consistency and expel trapped air

PYROMETRIC CONES — Sticks or pyramids of ceramic material which deform at a given temperature and are used to gauge heat at kiln temperatures

REDUCING or REDUCTION ATMOSPHERE — The creation of an oxygen starved atmosphere in the kiln during firing. This causes oxygen atoms to be drawn from oxides thus influencing body and glaze colour

RUTILE — Mineral giving a distinctive mottled appearance to a glaze

SAGGAR — Refractory box in which ware is set in the kiln for support and protection from combustion gases

SALT GLAZE — Achieved by throwing common salt into the hot firebox of the kiln when the highest temperature is reached. The sodium chloride decomposes and combines with the silica of the clay to form a thin glaze coating with an orange-peel texture

SGRAFFITO — Technique of incised decoration consisting of the application of a coloured slip to a leather-hard clay surface, then scratching through it to expose the body colour

SLAB-BUILT — Built from slabs of clay

SLIP — Clay mixed with water to a smooth liquid consistency, sometimes coloured with a colouring oxide, and used decoratively over the clay body

STONEWARE — High-fired vitreous body which is fired between 1 200°C and 1 350°C

TENMOKU — A high-fired reduced iron glaze, which varies in colour from black to red depending on the thickness of the glaze, obtained from the addition of about 10% iron oxide to the glaze

THROWING — Technique of making pottery on a wheel

WAX RESIST — Decorative technique of wax designs applied to pottery surface to repel subsequent applications of slip, glaze or liquid pigments

WEDGING — Working a plastic body to achieve consistency and expel trapped air

INDEX

Page numbers given in italics refer to chapters devoted to particular South African potters dealt with in this book.